BURPEE

AMERICAN GARDENING SERIES

WILDFLOWERS

Juliet Alsop Hubbard

MACMILLAN • USA

This book is dedicated to my parents, Joyce and Lee Alsop, who inspired and continue to share my love of gardening.

Macmillan
A Prentice Hall Macmillan Company
15 Columbus Circle
New York, New York, 10023

Library of Congress Cataloging-in-Publication Data

Hubbard, Juliet Alsop.
    Wildflowers / Juliet Alsop Hubbard.
        p.   cm.—(Burpee American gardening series)
    Includes index.
    ISBN 0-02-860036-3
    1. Wild flower gardening—United States.   2. Wild flow-
ers—United States.   3. Wild flowers—United States—Pictorial works.
    I. Title.   II. Series.
    SB439.H77   1995
    635.9'5173—dc20   94-5194
                                              CIP

Designed by Levavi & Levavi
Manufactured in the United States of America

10   9   8   7   6   5   4   3   2   1

Burpee is a registered trademark of W. Atlee Burpee and Company.

Photography Credits:
Alsop, Joyce
Bales, Suzanne
Silva, David

I would like to express my appreciation to the following people for the various roles they played in making this book a reality: Marjorie Williams, Joyce Alsop, Lee Alsop, Susan Greenstein, Janet Stoliker, Bill Osborn, Annabelle Lee, Anne Bevans, Keith Neer, Alexa Venturini, Calista Washburn, Wayne Winterrowd, Rebecca Atwater, Rachel Simon and, most importantly, my husband, John Hubbard.

Preceding pages: A clear pink selection of the native Cardinal flower, Lobelia 'Rose Beacon' combines beautifully with dusty miller, 'The Fairy' rose and ornamental alliums in the Connecticut garden of Fred and Mary Ann McGourty.

CONTENTS

INTRODUCTION

There is something so romantic about the idea of growing wildflowers. The mere thought holds associations of light and air and grass blowing gently in the wind. It brings me a sense of freedom and harmony with the natural world as I remember past excursions and quiet walks. By growing some North American wildflowers in your own garden, you too can evoke fond memories of seeing those same plants growing wild and free.

A garden of wildflowers is, in the truest sense of the term, a cottage garden. The original cottagers of old Europe had little money and no access to foreign and exotic plants. Instead, they dug the showiest of their local wildflowers from the surrounding fields and forest and placed them in the gardens around their homes, intermingling them with herbs and fruits and vegetables. If someone came across an unusual form of a wildflower such as a double-flowered specimen or one with a different colored blossom, that curiosity would be dug and divisions offered to friends and relatives. We continue that centuries-old tradition of cottage gardening when we include some of our local wildflowers in with our herbs, vegetables and other flowers.

As I weed and deadhead around the wildflowers in my garden, I experience moments of flag-waving patriotism as I recall that nearly one-half of my garden flowers were "Born in the U.S.A." Too often we fall back on the tried and true familiars—usually those native to Europe and Japan, such as vinca, pachysandra and hosta. I feel proud to be taking a leap and experimenting with combinations of wildflowers intermingled with more familiar garden plants.

I also feel a sense of history as I work around my wildflowers. The big bluestem grass (*Andropogon gerardii*) that I grow in my perennial borders once lined the sides of hundreds of miles of the Oregon Trail. Pioneer men and women spent weeks traveling in their Conestoga wagons through this giant, undulating grass. As I gaze at the pretty starlike blue flowers of the camassia that we now happily add to our spring gardens, I remember that these starchy bulbs were once an integral part of the diet of the Indian tribes of the Pacific Northwest.

Many of our wildflowers have intriguing common names that give us an idea of how they were used by Indians and early settlers. Names such as rattlesnake master (*Eryngium yuccifolium*) and maddog skullcap (*Scutellaria lateriflora*) call attention to the plants' medicinal use to treat snakebites and rabies. This adds a much broader dimension to gardening than merely combining colors and heights.

To some, wildflowers and the plants sold at garden centers seem worlds apart. They think of wildflowers as weedy and not showy, or else difficult to grow. What many people forget is that all plants are native to somewhere. Camellias grow wild in the woods in Japan and the sweet-scented mockoranges originated on the rocky hills of southern Austria and Italy.

Some American wildflowers have been grown for so long in "captivity" that we no longer remember that they once grew in the wild. The long-spurred columbines, which grace gardens throughout the world in spring with their delicate beauty, are native to the western half of the United States. The colorful garden phloxes that form a part of almost everyone's summer border can be found growing wild in rich woods in the eastern United States.

There are, however, a wealth of wildflowers—often unappreciated and overlooked—that are garden worthy and waiting to be discovered. Ahead we shall view some of these beauties.

*Shining coneflower (*Rudbeckia nitida 'Herbstsonne'*), willowleaf sunflower (*Helianthus salicifolius*) and cinquefoil (*Potentilla fruticosa*), in designer Suzanne Coe's late summer garden. This monochromatic color scheme is complemented by the variety of foliage shapes and textures.*

UNDERSTANDING WILDFLOWERS

When I first became acquainted with wildflowers, I found the subject rather awe-inspiring and even overwhelming. After all, the United States is enormous; it stretches over 3,000 miles from east to west and encompasses 8 plant hardiness zones ranging from completely frost-free areas to those with a mere 2 months of warm growing season. Contained within this great country are more than 100 different plant communities. I began my odyssey into the world of wildflowers by buying a simple pictorial wildflower field guide. But I wondered whether I could possibly learn about every plant listed in the book. Later on, of course, I discovered that I didn't have to.

I was quite fortunate to soon meet Joe Beitel, an extremely knowledgeable and enthusiastic field botanist. He quickly helped me put the giant world of wildflowers into a more understandable order. Through him, I learned that the easiest way to understand wildflowers was to familiarize myself with a few of my local plant habitats.

Each habitat is a specific ecological niche inhabited by a group of plants that have adapted to its particular characteristics of water, light and soil type. For instance, if you go to a beach or dune area, where there is plenty of sunlight, very sandy soil and little water because the rain percolates through the sand, you will find a repetition of the same dozen or so plant species throughout the area. Move to another local habitat such as a wood-land and again you will discover about a dozen plant species that compose the basis of this plant association.

Compartmentalizing wildflowers into habitats and their associated plant communities, made the whole learning process manageable. First, I learned about the plants of some of the most common habitats around me. I took my wildflower field guide and accompanied by my loyal Newfoundland dog (who sometimes would have preferred to stay home asleep), I began to comb the woods and fields right around my house. Anything that was pretty and caught my eye I looked up in my field guide. That is how my passion for "botanizing," as it is sometimes called, began.

Soon I made special trips to other interesting environs not immediately around my home. For instance, I journeyed to see the plants of the New Jersey Pine Barrens—a harsh, sandy, acidic habitat covering most of the southern half of New Jersey. There I saw two distinct plant communities based upon the land being dry or wet. The Pine Barrens is a beautiful place, but especially memorable on this trip was a long, peaceful afternoon I spent canoeing down a slow-moving stream, smelling the spicy fragrance of the sweet pepperbushes lining the stream's banks and seeing the white water lilies and blue pickerelweed flowers poking their faces up above the water's surface.

I now go out combing the land wherever I travel and always purchase a field guide to the

A glorious mix of skunk cabbage (Symplocarpus foetidus) *and tussock sedge grass* (Carex stricta) *alongside a stream in Easthampton, New York. The design is courtesy of Mother Nature.*

wildflowers of every spot in which I vacation. While you may never become an avid "botanizer," I should warn you that the compulsion can creep up on you—and before you know it you are caught.

Remember that although there are more than 100 different habitats and plant communities to be found across the United States, there will only be a few within your particular geographical area. It is those

you will want to know and will come to love. It is from those areas that you should first be seeking plants to include in your own garden.

THE RHYTHM OF THE SEASONS

As you spend time in the wild you will notice a distinct rhythm of bloom to the seasons. In the moister sections of the country, spring is the time of the woodlands as the forest-dwelling wildflowers put on their show. These plants are adapted to conditions of ample moisture in the soil from the melting snows and spring rains and to plenty of light filtering down through the leafless tree canopy above. The woodlanders grow quickly and flower in the early spring, taking advantage of the abundant sun and water. Many set seed promptly and even go dormant as the forest floor turns dry and the tree leaves emerge, blocking the sun.

In summer the display of flowers turns to the fields and prairies. Adapted to a long season of sunshine and sufficient moisture, these wildflowers take their time to grow and blossom, beginning the show in early summer and often continuing into the fall.

Color returns to the forest in autumn, as the leaves change to the vibrant shades of red, orange and yellow that make the eastern United States so famous.

In drier regions of the United States, blooming occurs soon after the winter and early spring rains. Some of the wildflowers have adapted themselves to be drought-avoiders. These plants have an annual life cycle. They germinate after

the rains and flower and set seed before the ground becomes parched and dry. Annuals such as orange and yellow Mexican poppies and blue lupines create a dramatic show in spring in Arizona, while golden yellow sweeps of tidy tips and goldfields attract tourists from miles around to the coastal ranges of California.

The majority of the perennials in drier regions also flower in the spring when there is sufficient water to support the production of flowers and seed. These perennials have adapted to the strong sun and dry conditions of the summer and autumn by having either tap roots that reach deep into the soil for water or a wide-spreading net-

Acres of toothworts (Dentaria laciniata) *carpet a spring woodland in Ithaca, New York. These forest beauties take advantage of the abundant sun and water in spring to grow, flower and set seed before going dormant during the darker and drier days of summer.*

In moister sections of this country, summer is the time when the meadow and prairie flowers put on their show. Here vervain (Verbena hastata), *Joe Pye weed* (Eupatorium maculatum) *and boneset* (Eupatorium perfoliatum) *bloom in August along the shore of a lake in Taghkanic, New York.*

work of roots near the surface that catch any available drop of moisture. Often these plants have small leaves that are covered with hairs or a latex to reduce water loss. Gray-leafed plants such as white sage (*Artemesia ludoviciana*) are indicative of adaptation to dry conditions. The gray appearance is actually created by thousands of hairs on the surface of the leaves that protect them from scorching in the sun and slow the rate of transpiration. Cacti are an extreme example of adaptation to drought. They have virtually no leaves and a tough latex-covered stem.

Much can be learned by observing nature. We should have realistic expectations of what our land can produce in terms of the type of plant growth and the season of bloom. In moister regions of the country, emphasis should be placed on woodland flowers in spring and on sun-loving wildflowers in summer and fall. In drier areas we should rejoice in the spectacular springtime explosion of annual flowers in all the colors of the rainbow; and during the dry seasons we should appreciate interesting foliage textures, shapes and shades of green and gray. Realize that much of the beauty of nature lies in the enjoyment of seasonal changes in flower and foliage colors and in the landscape itself.

In drier regions of the United States, a profusion of blooms follows the rains of winter and spring. Hillsides of California are commonly brightened by the reds and blues of Indian paintbrush (Castilleja species) and lupines (Lupinus species).

ALIEN PLANTS

It is important to understand that not every wildflower you see is native to the United States. Many of our most familiar wildflowers (Queen Anne's lace, chicory and yarrow, for example) originally came from other areas such as Europe and Asia. Like the human population, our wildflowers are composed of plants from North America as well as plants from countries throughout the world. Some escaped from gardens, some were deliberately introduced, and some came along with the fodder and bedding of animals imported to this country. Despite horror stories of a few alien species such as kudzu, water hyacinth and purple loosestrife taking over acres of land, most of the introduced species live quite harmoniously with our natives. The nonnative species that are now self-perpetuating wildflowers are often referred to as naturalized species. Although many naturalized species are beautiful in their own right, this book features American natives.

WILDFLOWERS: THE FORGOTTEN PERENNIALS

If you were to research the country of origin of many favorite perennials, you would find that most come from other lands. Beloved flowers such as delphiniums and foxgloves originated in Europe, and balloon-flowers and daylilies come to us from Asia. Does this mean that North America has very few beautiful wildflowers of its own? Of course not.

To understand what has happened, one must reflect on the history of our young nation. The first colonists were primarily from Europe. They brought the fruits, vegetables and herbs from home that they could depend upon for survival. They also brought seeds of the flowers that reminded them of home. Thus the plants we consider old-fashioned garden flowers—hollyhocks, delphiniums, foxgloves and forget-me-nots—are all European native plants.

Contrary to popular belief, goldenrod does not cause hayfever. It is ragweed, which often grows in the same meadow habitats and has less noticeable flowers, that is the true culprit. The showy yellow plumes of seaside goldenrod (Solidago sempervirens) add sunshine to the fall garden.

The Misunderstood Goldenrods

I have always admired the clear yellow of goldenrods. They bloom over a period of four months during the summer and can be found in every habitat from bog to mountaintop with flowers in various shapes from flat-topped to plumelike to vertical.

Contrary to common belief, goldenrods do not cause hay fever. It is the ragweed, which so often grows in the same area as goldenrod, that is the culprit. The pollen of ragweed is carried from flower to flower by the wind and this wind-borne pollen is what irritates our noses. The pollen of goldenrod, on the other hand, is carried from flower to flower by bees. Because the flowers of ragweed are green and barely noticeable, it is the nearby and showy goldenrod that has been blamed for hay fever.

Years ago, with no fears about its potential to cause allergies, I dug a pretty goldenrod from alongside the road on my mother's property and moved it to her garden.

There it grew beautifully and combined well with many of the fall asters. Delighted by my success, I dug another goldenrod with narrow leaves and moved it to a different section of the garden. In the first season it was quite pretty, but the following spring I found that the same plant had spread to cover an area of 100 square feet. Out it went into the compost pile!

There are more than 70 species of goldenrod native to the United States. Many are well behaved and deserving of a place in the garden, others are far too invasive. There is little written about those many goldenrod species, and this is what constantly piques my interest in wildflowers in general: There is so much room for experimentation and learning. Some gardenworthy species of goldenrod include: seaside goldenrod (Solidago sempervirens), showy goldenrod (S. speciosa) and an early flowering dwarf goldenrod (S. canadensis 'Golden Baby').

Bowman's root (Gillenia trifoliata) is a beautiful wildflower that is seldom grown in this country. It is an elegant plant that in spring bears a profusion of starry white flowers above glossy green foliage shaped like that of the Japanese maple.

The colonization of North America happened concurrently with European exploration and colonization throughout the world. Soon after a European nation entered a country and declared it as its own territory, universities sent botanists and nurseries sent plant collectors there to bring back samples and seeds of the new and exotic plants. Gradually the exotic species were introduced to commerce and gardeners began to cultivate those new plants.

If there is one character flaw all gardeners seem to share, it is the overwhelming desire to grow that which is new and exciting. I am just as guilty as the next gardener. Each winter I find myself anxiously poring over those first few pages of the seed and plant catalogs that describe the very newest hybrid plant or the exotic introduction from a faraway place. Gardeners in the 19th and early 20th centuries were no different from gardeners today.

Chrysanthemums and peonies arrived from Asia, marigolds and zinnias were found in Mexico and impatiens came to us from Africa. These new plants were eagerly purchased by enthusiastic gardeners. Today, these foreign flowers have become commonly grown and well-loved American garden plants.

Many of our wildflowers were overlooked in the flurry of excitement over the new introductions. The old saying, "The grass is always greener on the other side of the fence," held true in this situation as the common flowers of our fields and forests were neglected upon the arrival of the new exotics.

Our wildflowers were not ignored everywhere. To Europeans, American wildflowers were just as interesting as plants from anywhere else in the world. Thus in Europe some of our native flowers such as the garden phlox and the monardas and lupines have been bred and improved upon for dec-

ades. We now import these improved cultivars of our own wildflowers with titles such as Monarda 'Blaustrumpf' ("blue stocking" in German) and the Russell hybrid lupines named after the gardener in Yorkshire, England, who crossbred several species of western American lupines to produce flowers in many color forms and combinations.

My insatiable desire for new and garden-worthy plants has fueled my interest in wildflowers. Before us we have a virtually untapped source of new garden plants that can be found in the woods and fields right around our homes.

Many American wildflowers are more appreciated abroad than they are at home. Our native monardas, for example, are popular in Germany. German growers have introduced a number of good color forms including 'Blaustrumpf' or 'Blue Stocking', which we now import to this country.

GIVE WILDFLOWERS A CHANCE

Don't be too quick to dismiss a newly found wildflower as being unworthy of a place in the garden. You must realize that in nature, plants are in constant competition with other species and may not necessarily be performing to the best of their ability. Consider that a plant will germinate wherever chance has allowed its seed to fall. It may be a rocky spot underneath another plant where the flower must lean way out to get light to grow. Under these tough conditions, the plant may be able to produce only a few sparse flowers. If you move it to a garden and give it better conditions—slightly improved soil and sufficient space in which to grow—it is quite likely that the same plant will reward you with a great outpouring of blooms. Such is the case of the five-foot-tall, flat-topped white aster, (*Aster umbellatus*). In the wild it is not all that showy, but in the garden it produces abundant blossoms throughout the month of August that provide a lovely foil for many other late summer flowers.

You should also be aware that horticulturists can seek improved selections of wildflowers that are more deserving of space in our gardens. Larger flowers, different color forms, smaller size and distinct fall color are all traits that may be selected, which can take a so-so wildflower and turn it into a must for the flower border.

Do not be too quick to judge a flower in the wild. On their own, plants must compete for soil, water and light. This flat-topped white aster (Aster umbellatus) grows from an infertile rocky crevice alongside a lake in Maine and reaches out over the water for sunlight. When brought into a more hospitable garden setting, this same aster rewards the gardener with an cloud of blossoms in late summer.

AVAILABILITY

Wildflowers continue to gain popularity. Over the past 10 years I have watched many nurseries and mail-order distributors pop up all over the country specializing in local plants. As demand increases it will become easier and easier to find your local wildflowers, but in the meantime it may require a little research and perseverance to locate the plants you want. Begin by contacting your local botanical garden or wildlife center and cooperative extension agency. See page 91 for a list of nurseries from which you can order wildflowers.

DESIGNING WITH WILDFLOWERS

Knowledge of a few of your most common local plant communities and associations can make the initial development of a garden plan easier. Do you live on a windy, dry hilltop, or perhaps beside a stream in a low, moist site? Which local wildflowers commonly grow in similar situations in your area? What natural combinations often occur together in such a site? This can be a starting point in your design. When I am designing a planting, the ecological plant association I choose becomes the basis for the rest of my design. It defines the "look" of the planting.

For example, if I were gardening in the midst of an open field, I would begin by thinking of the wildflowers I commonly find growing in such a situation. First, I would select some grasses, for it is their fluid movement and strong vertical blades that define the meadow. Secondly, I would consider the wildflowers most commonly found with those grasses. Then I would analyze the various plants as a whole—in terms of height, how aggressively or weakly they grow, their time of bloom, shapes and texture and color.

You don't have to confine yourself solely to the plants found in your area. An argument I hear quite often is that because wildflowers evolved in a certain region of the country they are best adapted to its particular climatic conditions and so those plants should be grown in the gardens of that area. This argument sounds convincing but is not always correct. Some wildflowers such as the Indian paintbrush, eriogonums and orchids are difficult to establish and grow in a garden setting and are better left to the specialist grower or to grow on their own in the wild. Other plants, such as some of the horsetails or *Equisetum* species, once introduced, are almost impossible to eradicate from a garden. Conversely, many nonnatives such as forsythia and daffodils perform well under a variety of climatic conditions and hold a well-earned position in our plantings.

You may desire more color and texture and a longer blooming season than is found in a particular habitat in nature. In that case, you may want to reach outside the confines of the local plant community and choose other plants that are native to similar habitats elsewhere in the United States or in other parts of the world.

For instance, in a dry, exposed spot I like to contrast the lacy, silver leaves of beach wormwood (*Artemisia stelleriana*), which comes from Japan, with the shiny green leaves of the native bearberry (*Arctostaphylos uva-ursi*). This planting looks appropriate because in each case the plants originated in similar dry, sandy habitats, albeit in different countries. It is fun to play with mixing flowers from all corners of the earth. However, be aware that if you ignore too many ecological principles, the plants will not perform well and the planting itself will not look right.

The meadow is the source of inspiration for this naturalistic planting of Joe Pye weed (Eupatorium purpureum), *New York ironweed* (Vernonia noveboracensis) *and sneezeweed* (Helenium autumnale) *in Suzanne Coe's Connecticut garden.*

Mini Habitats

Be aware that construction and backfill and the shadows from buildings can create mini-habitats within your small yard. For instance, most of my garden is in a wetland site with fairly rich gravelly soil and a stream meandering through it. The soil level around the house, however, was raised above the rest of the

yard to keep the basement from flooding. The fill used to create this higher plane is an infertile sandy gravel that holds no water. This small area is better suited to plants from a beach and dune setting than to plants found in the moist fields and woods immediately surrounding the house.

Never let yourself be paralyzed into inactivity by recommendations to study textbooks carefully and to plan everything on paper. The actual time you spend outdoors digging in the dirt and observing the growth habits and performance of a perennial in your garden is just as important as the desk work. With familiarity comes the confidence to design more artistically and successfully. Don't be afraid—it is important to know and grow the plants. Do not expect perfection in your first garden. Even veteran gardeners are constantly making changes and adjustments to their seemingly perfect landscapes. It is this constant quest for perfection that makes gardening a hobby for life. On the other hand, a little bit of re-

search and planning can save you many years of effort and disappointment. Heed warnings of invasive plants and place them only where you don't mind them spreading freely. Follow recommendations for sun or shade. Sun lovers can often tolerate an hour or two of shade and shade plants can often take a few hours of sunlight, but if you completely ignore the plants' cultural requirements you are inviting disaster. Winter is the time I love to pore over picture books and magazines, look up information on individual plant species and draw elaborate plans for future gardens and renovations. To me that is almost as much fun as the actual gardening during the growing season.

COLOR IN THE WILDFLOWER GARDEN

When combining colors within a garden it is useful to remember a few basic concepts of color theory. The relationship of colors to one another is represented frequently by the color wheel. The "warm" colors—red, orange and yellow—form one-half of the wheel, and the "cool" colors—purple, blue and green—form the other half. Warm colors reach out and stimulate the eye, while cool colors are more soothing and recede from view. A planting of bright yellow, red and orange sunflowers would be quite a showy planting, while a combination of blue and lavender woodland phloxes would be more of a quiet planting.

As you place various colors together, remember that the colors opposite one another on the wheel (e.g., blue and orange, red and green, and purple and yellow) contrast with each other, and are called "complementary." Use of these complementary colors will attract attention and give brilliance to the planting. On the other hand, adjacent colors on the color wheel harmonize when placed together in a garden. For instance, shades of orange and yellow or variations of purple and blue often blend together in a quietly pleasing manner. Neutrals such as white flowers and gray foliage provide a good background for and en-

hance other colors. White also glows in the dark. This becomes an important consideration when planning a garden that will be viewed during the evening hours.

You must realize that a flower color is rarely a pure red or yellow. There are many tones to flower colors. Some yellows have orange in them, such as *Heliopsis helianthoides*, while others such as *Coreopsis verticillata* 'Moonbeam' are a pale yellow with greenish overtones. All too often, gardening books will only tell you that a plant is yellow, white, orange or red. Yet two red flowers may be worlds apart, with one almost orange and the other with strong purple tones. Sometimes photographs will help to clear up the picture, but by and large you have to observe variances of color by actually seeing the plant in bloom.

It is interesting to observe the blending of color in nature. Quite often one sees the combination of yellow and lavender in the wild. In the spring it is the purple-blue woodland phloxes with the celandine poppies. In summer, the lavender-colored *Monarda fistulosa* with early goldenrods or the yellow sunflowers and purple liatris carry on this theme. And in fall, the later goldenrods and violet asters follow suit. This is an example of how two opposites on the color wheel can be very effective together. A simple combination that occurs in the summer is the bright red of the cardinal flower, growing in a moist and somewhat shady spot, framed by the greens of ferns and skunk cabbage foliage. This, too, is an example of contrasting colors.

The bright reds, yellows and oranges of autumn leaves make a spectacular and also beautiful display because all of those colors are in harmony with one another. If you were to check, you would find that they are all adjacent colors on the color wheel.

My favorite way to design with color is to combine various tones of the same color, such as blue, with a single contrasting color, such as yellow. Thus in a shade garden I often combine the blue woodland phlox, which can be found in several tones of blue and blue-purple, and paler blue polemo-

In the wild, the lavender pink of Joe Pye weed (Eupatorium purpureum) *and the greenish yellow of the goldenrod* (Solidago *species) and cut-leaved coneflower* (Rudbeckia laciniata) *demonstrate a naturally effective use of complementary colors.*

nium with the yellow celandine poppy. A variation on this theme in the late summer border might have several forms of the helenium in reds and oranges with the blue *Scutellaria incana.*

When planning for color in the garden, consider timing. Most flowers are in bloom for only about four weeks of the year, so you will need to determine bloom time as well as the color of each flower in order to create the desired effect. Although planning for an entire season of color combinations may seem overwhelming at first, it actually frees you to play with different colors throughout the seasons. For instance, the spring garden might feature cooler blues, yellows and whites, while the late summer and fall garden can showcase warmer reds, yellows and blues. Gardens are not static— they change every day, week, month and year. This is what makes them so exciting.

Pretty Color Combinations by Season

Spring: Blue woodland phlox (*Phlox divaricata*) with the yellow wood poppy (*Stylophorum diphyllum*) and the lyre-shaped fronds of maidenhair fern (*Adiantum pedatum*)

Summer: Lavender Joe Pye weed (*Eupatorium purpureum*) and magenta New York ironweed (*Vernonia noveboracensis*) with the lemon yellow of shining coneflower (*Rudbeckia nitida*)

Summer: The golden yellow of black-eyed Susan (*Rudbeckia fulgida*) and the bright orange of butterfly weed (*Asclepias tuberosa*) against a backdrop of green grass such as little bluestem (*Andropogon scoparius*)

Autumn: the coppery inflorescences of Indian grass (*Sorghastrum nutans*) and the sunny yellow blossoms of hairy gold aster (*Chrysopsis villosa*) against a clear blue sky

FOLIAGE: THE BACKBONE OF THE GARDEN

Flowers and color are what initially attract most people to gardening. A few years of designing a garden purely on the basis of color, however, will show you that flowers alone do not a garden make. I had to

The brown cones and reflexed yellow petals of prairie coneflower (Ratibida pinnata) *are supported by fine stems to a height of 4 feet. This plant creates a light and airy effect in the garden.*

The spiky inflorescences of fairy candles (Cimicifuga racemosa) *provide a strong vertical accent in the perennial garden designed by Lynden Miller at the New York Botanical Garden.*

Ostrich fern (Matteuccia struthiopteris) *quickly forms a beautiful colony in a damp and shady site. In addition to this fern's usefulness as a groundcover, its young fiddleheads may be harvested for a gourmet treat in spring.*

prove it to myself, but after many years of experimenting, I now realize that foliage texture and contrast form the backbone of the border. Flowers are merely transient spots of color highlighted by the leaves around them. They are still very important to me, but I use foliage to emphasize the beauty of flowers. If you observe natural stands of wildflowers, you will find that the blossoms are always made more beautiful by a backdrop of grasses or a lichen-covered rock.

Once I have defined the "look" or habitat upon which I am basing a particular design, be it meadow, mountaintop or woodland, I begin by placing the anchoring or backbone plants that will tie together the garden. Often I repeat the same plant or plants with a similar effect periodically throughout the garden. I always base my selection of these key plants on their foliage texture and shape and their architectural habit of growth. Architectural plants are those whose foliage or branching habit provides interest of a more permanent and solid nature than the ephemeral color of flowers.

In this category of architectural plants fall many shrubs, ferns and grasses as well as other plants with bold foliage or growth habits. A smaller shrub such as shrubby cinquefoil, (*Potentilla fruticosa*), with its finely cut, gray-green foliage and delicate white or yellow summer flowers, or grasses with strongly vertical lines such as Indian grass (*Sorghastrum nu-*

tans), work well in sun. The big maplelike leaves and lavender-pink blossoms of the flowering raspberry (*Rubus odoratus*), or the giant goat's beard (*Aruncus dioicus*), which looks like a five-foot-tall astilbe, provide good contrast in the shade garden.

After the backbone plants have been placed, it is time to pick from several other categories of growth habit. I usually place plants into the following groups:

- ◆ Plants that are light and airy looking, such as the prairie coneflower (*Ratibida pinnata*) with its long, fine stems above which rise many rocketlike flowers, or wand flower (*Gaura lindheimeri*), a native of Texas, which blossoms for months with a multitude of dainty, starlike white flowers.
- ◆ Wildflowers that make strongly vertical statements, such as liatris or blazing-stars with their lavender spikes, or the tall, pitchforklike inflorescences of *Cimicifuga racemosa*, which can appear quite eerily from a shady corner.
- ◆ Plants that form low mounds in the garden—some of the June-flowering phlox species such as *Phlox glaberrima* or *P. pilosa*, for example, have pink blossoms that completely cover 15-inch plants. Several of the fall-blooming New York aster cultivars also form low mounds well suited to placement in the foreground of a garden.

PLANTS THAT TIE A GARDEN TOGETHER: BLENDERS AND SELF-SOWERS

Once the garden is established, I like to see some of the plants running into one another. I also like to have a few flowers seed themselves about and mingle among the defined groupings; this unifies a garden and gives it a more natural and established feel. One of my favorites is *Lobelia siphilitica*, which produces many blue spikes in late summer and fall. The plant seeds itself about but is easy to pull up when unwanted. In the spring when I am weeding I simply decide if the blue would be a nice addition in this particular spot. If it would be, then I leave it; otherwise, I take out a cultivator or trowel and scratch up the new seedling.

The yellow flowers of the wood poppy (*Stylophorum diphyllum*) provide a similar blending effect in the woodland garden.

Phlox stolonifera will creep along the ground around other perennials at a rapid rate. I have seen it used very effectively in a perennial border where it was permitted to cover the areas under the feet of the taller, later-blooming perennials. In spring it sent up many pink and blue flowers while the other plants were just starting to grow. Interspersed among the phlox were some of the smaller bulbs such as snowdrops, grape hyacinth and scillas. The phlox extended the bloom season of this garden

Tiers of whorled leaves along 6-foot stems and dome-shaped clusters of dusty rose flowers make Joe Pye weed (Eupatorium maculatum) a focal point of Joyce Alsop's late summer and fall garden. Taking inspiration from the meadow setting of its origin, the Joe Pye weed is combined here with the vertical lines of an ornamental miscanthus grass.

into early spring, while the taller perennials provided the leaves of the phlox with their necessary shade during the summer months.

PLACING THE PLANTS

Taking your inspiration from nature, plant groups or drifts of the same flower rather than dotting individuals around the garden. Don't be too uniform though, because that can look stiff and formal. It is wise to repeat either the same plant or plants with similar form rhythmically through the garden to create continuity and logic to the design. That way the garden looks put together like a well-dressed person, not a hodgepodge of completely unrelated fashion statements. Even an eclectic combination needs some kind of theme to tie it together.

For instance, when I designed a fall-flowering border for my September wedding, I used several types of ornamental grasses periodically in the background, the center and foreground to tie the design together. I also regularly interspersed the tall New England asters in the back, the dwarfer cultivar 'Alma Potschke' in the middle, and the dwarf New York asters in mounds along the front. These flowers all share a similar daisy shape and bloom in colors ranging from pale pink to hotter pinks to lavenders and purples. Through their repetition, the grasses and asters helped give

the essentially natural and meadowlike border a sense of design and order.

Great blue lobelia (Lobelia siphilitica) seeds itself generously around the garden. Its sky-blue color complements many other flowers such as this red daylily. The repetition of the lobelia's vertical spikes can also unify a planting.

DEMYSTIFYING XERISCAPING

Yuccas and opuntias are examples of drought-tolerant, evergreen plants that provide an aesthetic, low-maintenance solution for dry, sunny gardens.

The word *xeriscaping* can be a little intimidating—it sounds very high tech. However, it is just a term to define any garden planned around a conservative use of water and the selection of plants that don't require an exorbitant amount of irrigation. Actually, it is just common-sense gardening. Every garden requires some watering in the first season as the roots of the plants expand deeper and wider into the soil from the tiny pot shape in which they came. Until they have developed a good, extensive root system, they need watering. However, we should all be selecting plants that will not require much extra watering once they are established, rather than plants that demand lots of water. This makes sense both ecologically, because we should not waste a valuable resource, and financially, because the water bill can add up quickly in the summer months. Also, who really wants to spend all weekend dragging hoses and setting up sprinklers? The obvious answer is to choose drought-tolerant plants.

An intelligent choice in drier regions of the country is a big spring show of annuals such as California poppies with phacelia, which form a tapestry of blue and orange. Architectural drought-tolerant plants such as cacti, yucca and mosquito grass will provide a quieter background planting for these bright flowers. This garden can be mulched with local pebbles, particularly in the annual areas. When the annuals finish their performance, the stones make a good surface for collecting and holding the annual seeds until the following winter's rains cause them to germinate. The pebbles also serve to accentuate the other permanent plantings.

You can stretch your water supply by channeling the runoff from roofs and other surface areas to fan out to your garden beds. I find this garden level of hydraulic engineering to be endlessly fascinating. I can spend hours, if not days, making channels and undulations in the landscape to redirect water flow. In fact, it is almost as absorbing as watching another person work (something that seems to be a universal pleasure).

MEADOWS

No other form of wildflower gardening has received as much attention and press coverage recently as the meadow. All too often, meadows have been touted as the easy, low-maintenance answer to lawns and gardens. This most definitely is not the case.

When people see a photograph of a meadow in a magazine or an ad, they believe that is the way their landscape will look for at least 6 months out of the year, year after year. Most photographs are of annual meadows composed primarily of such nonnatives as Flanders poppy and bachelor's buttons. They flower for about 2 months, set seed and die. In most regions of the United States the seeds will not survive to germinate next year and that is the end of the display. Unless the site is prepared well and all weeds are removed through the use of repeated tillings or herbicides, the meadow can quickly become a weedy disaster. The lack of proper soil preparation and the annual nature of most meadow seed mixes are the most common reasons for failure and disappointment.

In most regions of the country, a natural meadow is composed of a lot of grasses punctuated by flowers blooming periodically throughout the season. There is not a constant barrage of color, but rather a quieter sort of beauty with each individual blossom highlighted by the background of vertical grasses. If you are looking for a brilliant burst of color, choose an annual flower meadow. Make sure you remove the weeds and plan to resow the meadow every spring.

A perennial meadow is more complicated to establish. Many of the perennial flowers and grasses take several years to mature. A cover crop may be needed to hold the soil and to provide some shade for the young wildflower seedlings. The selection of appropriate seed for your area, the type of cover crop, proper preparation of the soil, time of planting, and so on are best left to a professional. Perennial meadows are definitely worth having, and they have been particularly successful in the prairie states, but this is a project that needs a great deal of research and thought before sowing.

Sometimes you can increase the flowering and performance of an existing meadow by varying your maintenance regime. For instance, if you want a lower meadow that flowers with a few alien but very pretty species such as daisies (*Chrysanthemum leucanthemum*) and Queen Anne's lace (*Daucus carota*) then you should encourage the production of seeds of these plants and weaken other plants that might compete with them. For daisies and Queen Anne's lace, you can do this by mowing in late June or early July, soon after they have blossomed. The other late-blooming flowers that are often more vigorous are severely set back by this mowing. The earlier-flowering daisies and Queen Anne's lace, denied the chance to set seed, usually respond to the cut by blossoming again and producing their seed in the fall.

The meadow surrounding my nursery is a very wet one. When I first moved here I was told by a local farmer that it was always mowed twice a year, first around the Fourth of July and once again in late October. I decided to encourage the late summer and fall blooming flowers that typically inhabit moist meadows in my area, such as Joe Pye weed, goldenrod, vervain, pink milkweed, turtlehead and asters. I omitted the July mowing and have been rewarded with an annual increase of these late bloomers in August and September.

I don't expect the meadow to be a sea of color for most of the year; instead, I await its autumn season of glory. During the other months I enjoy the occasional penstemon or black-eyed Susan highlighted by the graceful moving grasses. It is low maintenance, requiring only one mowing a year, but it is not a showplace. I wouldn't turn my front lawn into this kind of meadow, but I know the field is home to wildlife (bluebirds, for example) and that alone is enough to make it worthwhile for me.

You can emulate the beauty and grace of a meadow in the garden by selecting the most gardenworthy meadow plants. Keep in mind the importance of the undulating, vertical grasses and include large clumps of them in your plan. Among the grasses of varying height and texture, place a variety of appropriate meadow wildflowers, which provide bloom throughout the growing season. A selection of grasses might include big bluestem, In-

A prairie planting at the Matthaei Botanical Garden in Ann Arbor, Michigan, features the lavender spikes of leadplant (Amorpha canescens), *purple coneflowers* (Echinacea purpurea) *and the bold foliage of prairie dock* (Silphium terebinthinaceum).

The quiet display of a typical dry meadow in the East includes butterfly weed (Asclepias tuberosa) *and black-eyed Susan* (Rudbeckia hirta).

dian grass and switch grass in the background, with stands of mosquito grass and prairie dropseed in the foreground. Among these grasses you might choose to place penstemons, dodecatheons, rudbeckias, helianthus, ratibidas, liatris or Joe Pye weed. This more carefully designed meadow garden would certainly be worthy of a place in your front yard. Of course, it would require the typical care and grooming needed by all perennial gardens to look neat throughout the seasons.

THE WILDFLOWER PLANTING AND GROWING GUIDE

In most respects, the planting and care of wildflowers is no different than that of other plants. After all, all plants originated someplace in the world. Forsythia grows wild in Asia and geraniums grow freely in South Africa. Once you realize that all plants grow wild somewhere, you should be less intimidated by the idea of growing your local flowers.

After you have selected your plants and designed your new garden, the preparation and planting techniques will be the same as in any perennial garden. The first thing you will need to do is to strip off the sod or weeds that are currently growing in the site. I usually use a mattock or a sod stripper to do this. Next, turn over the soil with a digging fork, spade or rotary tiller to one spade's depth. I have found double digging unnecessary; all of my plants grow quite well in single-dug beds (I will make an occasional exception for a particular clematis or some other deep-rooted plant). Remove rocks as you dig. If you are using a rotary tiller, double-check the depth to which it is digging. Some machines are remarkably thorough, while others merely "walk" across the top 2 inches of the bed. In the latter case, get out your spade, hire a strong person, or find a better rotary tiller.

In the process of digging you will discover a lot about your soil. Generally speaking, soils can be lumped into 3 types: sand, loam and clay. If you squeeze moist soil in the palm of your hand and it will not clump together, then you have a sandy soil. Sandy soil does not hold moisture well because it is quite porous. If, on the other extreme, the soil clumps together tightly and will not break apart, then you have clay. A clay soil is rich in nutrients, but water will not drain well and plants can suffer from lack of oxygen. When the clay does dry out it becomes hard like a brick. Plants find it difficult to grow roots in this kind of soil. Loamy soil is somewhere between the two. It will form a loose clump when squeezed but can also be crumbled back to its original texture. This is closer to the ideal soil texture.

The three soil types all benefit from the addition of organic matter such as compost, rotted manure or peat moss. Adding organic matter to your soil is just as important as adding vegetables and grains to your own diet. The bulky coarseness of organic matter creates more air and drainage space in clay soil. And organic matter also helps sandy soil to hold more moisture and nutrients. Spread the soil amendments over the surface of the garden to a depth of several inches. Turn this into the soil with a digging fork, spade or rotary tiller. Once the amendments have been mixed in, smooth and grade the surface of the ground with a soil rake.

The cup plant (Silphium perfoliatum) *and giant coneflower* (Rudbeckia maxima) *are two examples of wildflowers with a dramatic presence in the garden.*

MAKING A COMPOST PILE

Creating your own "black gold" or compost is an integral part of the gardening process. It always amazes me to see how much organic material a garden can produce in a single season. Weeds, deadheaded flowers, stems of perennials cut back in fall and leaves from trees combine to form quite a pile of organic debris by winter. Since gardens and gardeners never seem to have enough compost, the obvious answer is to continually compost the organic matter from your own plantings. Composting can be as simple as creating an enormous pile of debris and leaving it to decay for several years. This method is easy but it requires a big yard where space is not a consideration, for the pile can become quite large over a period of years. Not a beautiful sight, it is best placed where it can be screened from general viewing.

Many people don't have huge amounts of space to devote to a compost pile. In this case the best solution is to build a small fenced off enclosure to contain the organic matter and to manage the pile so as to speed up the rate of decomposition. Constant moisture and air are essential to the decomposition process. It is easiest to keep the pile moist if it is placed in a shady location. The fence used to hold the compost should allow air to pass through to the pile. Many gardeners use sturdy chicken wire as fencing for this reason. It is a good idea to add several inches of soil periodically to the pile. Soil naturally contains the bacteria needed for decomposition. A few cups of ground limestone can be added at the same time to help keep the pH at the optimum level for bacterial activity. Chopping up leaves and stems of plants into smaller sizes will also speed up the composting process. To further help aerate the compost and speed up decomposition you should plan to turn the pile every month or so. Do not add plants that have been treated with herbicides to the pile. Kitchen scraps are fine, but meat and bones are best thrown in the garbage so as not to attract foraging animals and complaints from the neighbors.

The annual addition of organic matter is part of the natural cycle of birth, growth and death in the wild. Every autumn, leaves and needles drop from the trees and cover the soil with an organic mulch. This mulch protects plants from extremes of temperature in the winter and it helps to conserve water and keep roots of plants cooler in the summer. The leaves gradually decay during the year, releasing small amounts of nutrients in the form of organic matter into the soil. Worms play an important role in the soil-making process because they take organic matter from the surface and bring it down deeper in their many tunnels. These same tunnels also serve to aerate and lighten the soil, allowing oxygen and water to pass more freely through the earth.

One needn't turn every garden spot into the perfectly prepared site for a vegetable or rose garden. If you have designed and selected your plants wisely (acid-loving plants in an acid site and plants from sandy sites for the beach house, for example), then you should only need to improve the soil to a limited extent. However, it always helps to dig some organic matter such as well-rotted manure or compost into the soil. The plants will grow faster, require less water and flower better with the additional nutrition and "fiber."

This compost starter bin is easy to make from four 4-foot posts, set in a rectangle, wrapped in chicken wire. If the chicken wire is secured loosely on the fourth side, the bin can be opened easily for removal of compost or for working the compost pile.

PLANTING

The ideal time to plant is early or late in the day when the sun is low, or on a cloudy, slightly drizzly day. Beware of windy, cloudy days: Wind can be just as stressful to plants as the sun. Make sure all plants are well watered before planting. This gives you some time to set out the plants and make adjustments to your design without worrying about the plants drying out. As you double-check your design, keep in mind the ultimate size of the plants at maturity, their time of bloom, flower color and leaf shapes.

To plant a container-grown wildflower in the garden, "knock" the plant out of its container by turning it on its side or upside down, while holding the soil around the base of the plant with one hand. Gently tease the roots, pulling them out of the pot-shaped growth habit. This is very important: By wounding the roots and pulling them into a slightly different pattern, you

encourage them to branch and grow into the soil outside the container shape. Unteased roots tend to keep growing around and around the original plug of soil in which they were first grown. More root-bound plants and some container-grown shrubs may require taking a knife and scoring the sides of the root balls to injure the roots slightly and encourage side-branching out into the planting hole.

Dig a hole that is twice as wide as the size of the root system. Place the plant in the hole. Make sure the top of the soil around the plant is at the same height as the surrounding soil (add more soil to the hole if the plant is too deep, enlarge the hole if the plant sticks up above the ground). Make sure the plant is straight in the hole. Fill in soil about halfway up the rootball. Tamp it down firmly with your hand (or your foot, for very large plants). Press firmly enough to get out any air

pockets; you want soil to be in contact with all of the roots. On the other hand, do not press so hard that you have created a layer that is impenetrable to air and water. Fill in the remaining half and tamp again.

When planting divisions of transplants, you can still spend some time placing and redesigning. Just make sure the plants are well watered and covered with moist burlap or some other breatheable material to help reduce moisture loss. Do not use plastic because it will act like a mini-greenhouse and cook your plants in the sun. Keep an eye on the divisions and watch for any sign of stress and wilting. Plant them as soon as possible just as you would the potted plants, except you won't need to tease the roots because the roots of these plants have not been confined to pots. Water each division immediately after planting to avoid stress due to the shock of transplanting.

MULCH

Nature never intended for earth to be left uncovered. All places in the wild, except a newly eroded site or a recent volcano, have some sort of blanket over the soil. Either there are plants growing on top of the ground, as in a meadow, or there is a layer of leaves, as one sees in the forest. Even in winter, the foliage of the previous season's grasses and flowers drapes over the soil, protecting it from erosion. Too often, people are blind to this

basic fact—the most dramatic example of this in recent history was the depression-era dust bowl, which was caused by insufficient use of cover crops. Controlling soil erosion is just one reason to mulch. For the gardener, the most obvious benefit of mulching is that it greatly reduces the number of weeds, and saves hours of back-breaking weeding.

There are many types of mulches to use, from chopped leaves and buckwheat hulls to

In the woods, the umbrella-like shoots of mayapple (Podophyllum peltatum) *push their way through a natural mulch of fallen leaves. During the summer the leaves will gradually decay, adding nutrients to the soil.*

In this garden, woodchips were used to help stabilize the soil and retain moisture on a dry slope. A planting of prairie smoke (Geum triflorum) enjoys the cooler and moister soil provided by the organic layer of woodchips.

shredded bark and pebbles. The mulch you choose is a question of personal aesthetics, local availability and cost. For the most part I prefer organic mulches because they gradually break down and add nutrients to the soil. The presence of an organic mulch also seems to attract earthworms (worms help move organic matter deeper into the soil and create small tunnels for air and water movement). However, pebbles or gravel sometimes look more appropriate in a site. Although rocks do not add humus to the soil, they will control weeds and temperature fluctuations. Small stones or gravel can also be useful in erosion-prone sites.

WATERING

I like to water all plants (pot grown or transplants) before planting. That way I can set out all of the plants in the site, stand back for a while and fiddle with the design and then plant. I recommend watering the newly planted garden after putting down your mulch. Of course, if you can't get around to mulching within a few hours of planting, then the plants should be watered to prevent wilting and desiccation. However, if you mulch first, your job will be easier because you won't be tromping through mud with wheelbarrows and boots, which compacts the soil and makes a mess of yourself and the nice grading job you've done. Water on bare earth also tends to roll off and not soak into the soil. Water will percolate through a layer of mulch and disperse more gradually to the soil, which makes for better absorption and less runoff.

For the first season following planting, all of the wildflowers will require one *good* soaking per week. That means either a long, steady soaking rain of several hours or longer, *or* a good soaking by hose or sprinkler. The goal is to have the water trickle down to the full depth of the root balls. You want to encourage the growth of deeper roots so the plant is fully anchored in the ground and can withstand drought in future years. Even drought-tolerant plants will need this long soaking in the first year to get established.

During the second year you will need to soak the plants only during periods of extreme dryness. In following years, a well-planned garden should survive without any watering, although you may find that it will not always look its best without some occasional irrigation during a dry spell.

TRANSPLANTING

Never feel tied down by your design. If you are not happy with a particular plant combination, feel free to move the plants around. Generally it is best to move perennials in early spring or fall when the days are cooler and the plants are not in active growth. Begin by making sure the plant is well watered before digging, to lessen the shock of transplanting. Insert the spade straight down around the outermost leaves of the plant. Do not try to pry up the spade at all. Repeat this cutting process around the entire circle of the plant. For the next step it is usually best to have another person's help. Standing directly opposite one another across the plant, each person should insert a spade into the previous cut and pull the handle of the spade toward the ground. This will "pop" the plant up out of its hole. Lift the root ball gently out of the ground and place it on a piece of burlap. Never lift the plant by the foliage because the root ball may break apart. Carry the plant to its new home using the burlap as a sling. If it cannot be planted immediately, water the plant and place it in the shade to prevent it from wilting.

DIVISION

Some plants require division every 3 to 4 years in order to stay vigorous and happy, or because they have become too large for their site in the garden. For many plants, division is also a rewarding and economical way to increase the number of plants in your garden or to have gift plants to exchange with fellow gardening enthusiasts. To divide a plant, dig it up as if you were going to transplant it. Once the plant is out of the ground, insert two digging forks back to back in the center of the plant. As you pull the handles away from each other, the plant should gently separate into halves. If the plant is very large you may be able to repeat the process and divide the plants into quarters.

This is the textbook description of how to divide a plant. About half the time it is the method I use. Sometimes a particular plant (for instance one with a very dense, strong root system) needs another technique. An extreme example is when my husband and a friend tried to divide one of the bigger ornamental grasses. They inserted their forks as if the grass were any normal perennial, and began to pry the plant apart. Nothing happened. It soon became clear that something more brutal such as a sharp saw, serrated knife or even an ax was needed. Then when they tried to remove the forks from the roots of the grass, the forks wouldn't budge. For a while we thought the digging forks would have to remain a permanent

part of that grass planting. Finally, with four people tugging and pulling, we managed to remove the forks. I now think twice about dividing a big grass, and when I do I prepare for a struggle. On the opposite end of the spectrum is a plant such as the maidenhair fern (*Adiantum pedatum*), which has many delicate stems. These stems would be broken or damaged by a rough division with a digging fork. Instead, I make small cuts with a trowel and use my fingers to gently pry apart the roots and stems. Division requires a little common sense. Usually it is an easy, economical and rewarding way to increase the number of plants in your garden.

PRUNING

All shade-tolerant plants will grow better when given some dappled sunlight. They respond to several hours of filtered light by growing faster and more compactly and flowering more

profusely. The more light you can allow into a garden, the greater the selection of plants you will have from which to choose and the better they will perform. Usually, your options

for increasing sunlight are to remove a tree or to do some strategic pruning of the limbs of shrubs or trees. Pruning or tree removal is best done by a professional aborist.

FERTILIZING

Wildflowers benefit from a judicious application of fertilizer as much as any other garden plant. I am not a fan of overfertilizing a plant; it creates too lush a growth, often at the expense of flower production. Also, the additional stress placed on a plant can invite the attack of pests and diseases. On the other hand, a light fertilizing in

spring can encourage growth and flowers and make a new garden fill in more quickly.

Generally I use a low-nitrogen fertilizer such as 5-10-5. The percentage of nitrogen in a bag of fertilizer is indicated by the first number in the sequence. In this case the fertilizer contains 5 percent nitrogen. This is a good low number that will not

cause burning provided you follow the instructions on the bag. Avoid high numbers such as 20 or above. Those types of fertilizers should only be used on lawns. If you prefer to use organic alternatives, top dress the plants with a thin layer of compost each spring.

The seedpods of some plants such as the purple coneflower (Echinacea purpurea) remain ornamental all winter long. In addition to their beauty, the seeds provide food for hungry birds.

DEADHEADING

The removal of spent flowers is a personal maintenance issue. The production of seeds does take energy away from plant growth and future flower production, so sometimes it is worth removing spent blossoms. For example, I often deadhead my ox-eye sunflower (*Heliopsis helianthoides*) to encourage it to produce sunny yellow flowers all summer long.

On the other hand, I enjoy the shape of some seedpods, so I don't deadhead the flowers; instead I leave up the seedheads until spring to add some interest to the winter landscape. A few of my favorites in this category include black-eyed Susans, purple coneflowers, downy skullcap and ironweed.

Some plants will self-sow in the garden when allowed to go to seed. Experience will teach you which plants are a problem in your garden and which are desirable additions. Don't slavishly follow the advice of a book or another gardener—every garden is different. A weed in one garden may never self-sow in another. Cultural differences and exposure can greatly effect the performance of an individual plant. You will quickly learn which plants to deadhead immediately and which you will want to encourage to self-sow.

WINTER CARE

I always check the mulch on a bed before winter. If it looks a bit thin, I touch it up in the bare spots. Mulch is important in preventing temperature changes in soil. Extremes of melting and freezing during the winter months can cause plants to be heaved above the soil line. This heaving injures roots, but more importantly, the uplifted roots are exposed to the air and dry out within days. It is this desiccation which most quickly kills a plant.

Mulching limits the extremes of freezing and thawing and prevents a lot of heaving. It is still a good idea to walk around your garden periodically in winter and check for any signs of frost heave. Whenever you see a plant raised above the ground, gently push it back down with your fingers and tuck a bit of mulch around the base as an insulating blanket.

It is often wise to cover small plants that were planted in the fall with evergreen boughs. This provides them with even more protection. I usually do this after Christmas and use boughs cut from my Christmas tree. Wait until the ground is frozen to put the boughs on top. If you put the boughs down before the ground freezes you are providing an inviting shelter for mice. The idea is to keep the soil frozen until you remove the boughs in spring—that way the plant never thaws and has a chance to heave.

GROWING WILDFLOWERS FROM SEED

Most seeds are ripe for the picking when they turn a dark tan or brownish color. A ripe seed will usually either drop out of its pod when gently tapped or fall into your hand when brushed with a finger. Other ripe seeds may be contained within the fruit of berries, like those of the jack-in-the-pulpits (*Arisaema triphyllum*).

It is wise to research the plant you are going to propagate before you sow the seeds.

Some seeds should be sown immediately upon collection and never permitted to dry out. Many of the woodland wildflowers require this kind of treatment. These seeds are adapted to falling into the moist leafy duff of the forest floor and remaining there until winter's freeze. To prevent germination in midsummer (when the plant would not have enough time to grow suffi-

ciently before the harsh winter's cold), the seeds have a dormancy factor built into the seed coat that inhibits germination until the seed has been exposed to 3 months of warm and moist conditions and to at least 6 weeks of cool (40° F) and moist conditions. In nature the seed will have been "stratified," as it is called, during the winter months and the embryo within will be ready to germinate the following spring. Many of the meadow or prairie flowers, on the other hand, do not mind drying out after they fall to the ground. But they also require an extended period of moist cold, such as winter provides, before they germinate.

You can stratify your wildflower seeds in two ways. The easiest method, I find, is to sow the seeds in trays of a sterile seed mixture, just the way you would any annual or vegetable seed. Then cover them lightly with sterile sand and place the trays outdoors (protected from rodents) for the duration of the winter. Be sure to put them where you won't forget to water them in case there is a prolonged dry period. The seeds must be moist as well as cold for the stratifying to be successful. The following spring, when the temperature warms up, the seeds will germinate.

You can also sow the seeds in small containers filled with moist, sterile potting soil and enclose those containers in a plastic bag so they won't dry out. You then mimic the cold of winter by placing the containers in a refrigerator whose temperature is set around 40° F. for at least 6 weeks. Remove the plastic bag and move the containers to a warm area (70° F.) with plenty of indirect sunlight, or place them under artificial grow lights and await germination and growth.

You'll know that seeds of plants in the aster family are ripe if they fall into your hand when gently brushed with a finger.

Some seeds do not require any special pretreatment. Most annuals and plants originating in places with no winter cold will not require any stratifying to germinate. These plants only need to be sown and kept constantly moist, but not sopping wet, and they will germinate.

Sowing seeds requires patience. Most perennials will not bloom until the second or third growing season. It also requires vigilance because the tender young seedlings must never dry out or they will die instantly. On the other hand, you will be amazed at how quickly two or three years can pass by. It will seem like you just sowed the seeds when they are full grown and in blossom.

Sowing seeds also provides the gardener with an inexpensive way to have many plants and lots of extras for sharing. Sometimes you will find interesting variations cropping up within your seedlings—perhaps a white form or a very compact growing form. Who knows, you may have discovered a great new plant that may some day bear your name (e.g., *Aster* 'Jane Doe's Delight').

PLANT PORTRAITS

A large variety of North American wildflowers are discussed in detail in this chapter. Although there are many more lovely wildflowers that can be grown, these were selected on the basis of ease of cultivation, the availability of nursery-propagated (as opposed to wild-collected) stock, usefulness in the garden and beauty. Some of the featured wildflowers are already established garden favorites such as *Coreopsis verticillata* 'Moonbeam', while others such as *Porteranthus trifoliatus* and *Thalictrum polygamum* await popular discovery.

The Latin names may seem like a mouthful, but it is important to use the universally accepted system of nomenclature so that people in each region of the country can understand which plant is being discussed. The common name of a plant is often of local derivation. For example, what one person calls Virginia bluebells may be known as Virginia cowslip in another state. To avoid confusion it is wise to learn the botanical names of native plants as well as the common names.

The Latin, or botanical, name is based upon the system of classification developed by Linnaeus in the 18th century. The first name is the genus, a group of plants that share common attributes. The second name is the species, which denotes a specific subset or member of that group of similar plants. A variety is a naturally occurring form of a particular species, for instance, one with a white flower. Cultivars are plants that have desirable garden traits, such as an unusual color or habit of growth, and that gardeners have selected for continued propagation.

Common names, however, are fun to use and know. Often they are colorful or descriptive, like the name hairy beard-tongue for *Penstemon hirsutus*. In other instances they denote an historic use of the plant, like that of snakeroot for *Eupatorium rugosum*. All of the wildflowers in this chapter are listed under their Latin names and are cross-referenced by their common names. This chapter of plant portraits divides the entries into annuals, ferns, grasses and perennials.

PLANT PORTRAIT KEY

Here is a guide to the symbols and terms used throughout this section:

The Latin name of the wildflower is in boldface italic.

The phonetic pronunciation of the Latin name is in parentheses.

The common name of the wildflower is in boldface type.

Grade of difficulty: Wildflowers that take the least amount of care are identified as "easy." These plants are good choices for beginning gardeners. Moderately difficult to grow plants are identified as "moderate," and hard to grow plants are identified as "difficult."

The average hours of sun needed per day is indicated by symbols. The first symbol is what the plant prefers, but it is adaptable to all conditions listed.

The waxy gray-green leaves and lavender blossoms of showy beardtongue (Penstemon grandiflorus) *are a lovely addition to a dry garden in late spring.*

○ *Sun*　　　Six hours or longer of direct sunlight per day

◐ *Part shade*　Three to six hours of direct sunlight per day

● *Shade*　　Two hours or less of direct sunlight per day

There are also symbols for the following:

🌢 *Drought-resistant*
✳ *Heat-lover*
✲ *Cool-weather lover*
🌡 *Long-lasting cut flower*
❁ *Long bloomer (6 weeks or longer)*

Origin: Describes regions in which this plant may be found growing in the wild.

Habitat: Details the type of environment in which the wildflower naturally occurs, such as meadow or forest.

Height: These are for normal growth, but wildflowers provided with very fertile soil and a longer growing season could grow taller. Conversely, with poor growing conditions, the plant could be shorter.

Zones: The USDA Plant Hardiness Map of North America (page 92) is based on average annual temperatures for each area, or zone, of the United States and Canada. Check the map to find out which zone you live in. Some wildflowers grow better in northern gardens (Zones 3 to 6), some better in southern gardens (Zones 7 to 10) and a few will grow well anywhere. Every plant portrait lists the zones best for that plant.

Cultural information: Plants' preferences and information on how best to grow your plants are given here. We recommend the easiest and best methods of increasing your number of plants. Some perennials are best grown from seed, others from division or stem cuttings.

Recommended cultivars: We have recommended particular varieties or cultivars of wildflowers when there are choices available, to help you understand the differences among cultivars and to inform you about exceptional ones.

ANNUALS

Annuals are plants that grow, flower, set seed and die all within one season. Instead of using energy to produce extensive root systems and top growth, annuals pour their resources into flowers because the production of a vast quantity of seeds is what enables them to survive. Annuals are often the showiest and longest-blooming flowers, which makes them a useful addition to any planting.

The United States has many beautiful native annuals, many of which are found in the warmer and drier regions of the country. Annuals are ideally suited to this harsher environment. They can grow, flower and set seed during the moist season and then the seed will remain dormant in the soil during the heat and dryness of the summer and fall.

Sow annual seeds in early spring in most areas of the country. In warm regions, annual seeds may be sown in the fall. Sprinkle the seeds in the ground where they are to grow, since most resent being transplanted. Gently rake them into the soil and then tamp down lightly to press the seeds into the dirt. Keep the ground moist until the seeds have germinated and the seedlings are well established.

Clarkia amoena (KLAR-key-uh a-MOY-nah) **farewell-to-spring, godetia,** Easy. ○ 🌡
Origin: California
Habitat: Coastal bluffs
Height: 12 to 30 inches
Colors: Lavender, pink, white
Characteristics: The satiny pink, lavender or white blossoms of *Clarkia amoena* look lovely massed or included in a perennial border. This late spring and summer blooming plant does best in climates with cool summer nights and should be grown in full sun with moderate amounts of moisture. Breeders have developed many color forms and double and ruffled blooms as well. Clarkia also makes a useful plant for the cool greenhouse.
Cultural Information: Sow seeds where they are to be grown because they resent transplanting. Following germination, thin plants so they are spaced 6 to 12 inches apart. *Clarkia*

Clarkia amoena

amoena does best in cooler weather and should be sown in early spring in most of the country, but can be sown in early fall in Zones 9 and 10.

Uses: Annual and perennial gardens, cool greenhouses, cut flower.

California poppy; see *Eschscholzia*

Calliopsis; see *Coreopsis*

Coreopsis tinctoria (kor-ee-OP-sis tink-TOR-ee-ah) **calliopsis,** Easy. ○ 🔔

Origin: Western United States
Habitat: Dry fields
Height: 2 to 3 feet
Color: Yellow with a deep red-brown center
Characteristics: Calliopsis is found throughout the western half of the United States in sunny, dry grasslands. Its finely divided foliage with myriad golden yellow flowers makes it one of the most popular of the native annuals. It is also very easy to grow, blooming all summer long in virtually any site, provided it gets some sunshine.
Cultural Information: Sow the seeds of *Coreopsis tinctoria* where they are to grow, as they resent transplanting. Following germination, thin the plants to 6 to 8 inches apart.
Uses: Annual and perennial gardens, meadows, cut flower.

Eschscholzia californica (es-SHOAL-tzee-ah kal-i-FORN-i-kah) **California poppy,** Easy. ○
Origin: California
Habitat: Sunny fields and meadows
Height: 8 to 12 inches

Colors: Orange, yellow, white, mahogany
Characteristics: Given an occasional rain or sprinkle of water, the California poppy will bloom almost all season long. The orange-yellow species that grows in the wild is the most robust and long-lived in a garden setting. It will self-sow profusely, providing color year after year. The other color forms are sustained by gardeners carefully collecting seed and resowing each year. All colors are beautiful, highlighted against the finely divided, blue-gray mounding foliage. Very easy to grow, the California poppy prefers full sun and a well-drained soil.
Cultural Information: Eschscholzia californica resents being transplanted, so sow the seeds directly where they are to grow. Seeds may be sown in fall in the warmer climates of Zones 9 and 10 and in early spring in cooler areas. Thin plants to 6 inches apart.
Uses: Annual and perennial gardens, rock gardens, pots, window boxes.

Farewell-to-spring; see *Clarkia*

Godetia; see *Clarkia*

Helianthus annuus (heel-ee-AN-thus AN-you-us) **sunflower,** Easy. ○ 🔔
Origin: Western United States
Habitat: Prairies
Height: 2 to 12 feet
Colors: Orange, mahogany, yellow or cream with dark brown centers

Coreopsis tinctoria

Eschscholzia californica

Helianthus annuus

Characteristics: This is undoubtedly the most beloved of our wildflowers. It is the plant from which sunflower seed comes and it is extremely popular with children. Hybridizers have worked away at this species to produce everything from great 12-foot giants with 1-foot-wide flowers to dwarfer specimens bearing many smaller blooms.

Cultural Information: All forms should be sown in place once all chance of frost has passed. They should be thinned to 1 foot apart for the dwarfer varieties and 3 to 4 feet apart for the tall growing specimens. Grow sunflowers in full sun and a moderately rich soil.

Uses: Annual, perennial and vegetable gardens, cut flower, seed attracts birds.

Sunflower; see ***Helianthus***

FERNS

Gardeners tend to be seduced by color when choosing plants. Flower color is really just a fleeting statement in a garden. It is the texture, shape and color of leaves that defines a planting. If your garden does not look like the photos in horticultural journals, the problem may be a lack of textural contrast. Ferns are an essential structural component in a planting. With their grace, variety of shapes and sizes and ease of cultivation, they should be an integral part of all shade or damp gardens.

Despite their delicate appearance, most ferns are extremely rugged plants and easy to grow. A few are even quite invasive and should be used with care only where a vigorous groundcover is desired. The majority, however, are well behaved and highly ornamental perennials. Division in spring is the most satisfactory method by which to increase all ferns.

Adiantum pedatum (aye-dee-AN-tum pe-DAY-tum) **maidenhair fern,** Easy. ◑ ●
Origin: Northern United States
Habitat: Woodland
Zones: 3 to 8
Height: 2 feet
Characteristics: With its lyre-shaped fronds, blue-green leaves and contrasting dark stem, the maidenhair is probably the most popular of the wild ferns. It is found growing in fertile moist woods across the northern United States, but is highly adaptable to cultivation throughout most of the country, providing it receives partial shade and is grown in a rich, moist, organic soil. The plant slowly creeps, forming a nice colony or drift that reaches a height of 2 feet.
Cultural Information: Grow *Adiantum pedatum* in rich, moist soil in partial shade. Space young plants or divisions about 8 inches apart.
Uses: Shade or woodland gardens.

Cinnamon fern; see ***Osmunda cinnamomea***

Dryopteris (dry-OP-tear-is) **wood fern,** Easy. ◑ ●
Origin: Northern and eastern North America
Habitat: Rich woods and swamps
Zones: 3 to 9
Height: 2 to 4 feet
Characteristics: Many beautiful species and hybrids of the wood fern grow in swamps and rocky woodlands primarily of northern and eastern North America. All are garden-worthy plants, but only a few are commonly available. The evergreen *Dryopteris marginalis*, which grows to a height of 2 feet, is found on rocky hillsides. *D. spinulosa* is found in moist woods. It has a more incised and fancy leaf, which makes it popular for use in floral arrangements. *D. goldiana* is the giant of the group, with magnificent fronds that often reach a height of 4 feet.
Cultural Information: Both *D. marginalis* and *D. spinulosa* grow well in average garden soil in partial shade. Space them 18 to 24 inches apart. *D. goldiana* grows best in moist shady conditions and should be

Dryopteris spinulosa

Adiantum pedatum

spaced 24 to 30 inches apart.
Uses: Shade or woodland gardens. The fronds of *Dryopteris spinulosa* are used in cut-flower arrangements.

Interrupted fern; see *Osmunda claytoniana*

Maidenhair fern; see *Adiantum*

Matteuccia struthiopteris (ma-TWO-chee-ah strah-thee-OP-tear-is) **ostrich fern, Easy.** ◐ ●

Origin: Northern North America
Habitat: Swamps and wooded river edges
Zones: 3 to 8
Height: 2 to 5 feet
Characteristics: Ostrich fern is the only vase-shaped native fern that spreads by underground stolons or runners. When happy, the fronds can grow to a height of 5 feet, but they more commonly grow to 3 feet. Ostrich fern is an extremely vigorous grower, covering ground at a rapid rate. Put it in a constantly moist, shady position and you will be rewarded with big green fronds all summer and a lovely clear yellow color in fall. When planted in soil that dries out in summer, the fronds turn brown by midsummer and you will think the colony is dying. Although it will come back with vigor the next spring, the planting will look poor for much of the season in a dry site. Site it well and you will have a dramatic, low-maintenance groundcover. Another benefit of the ostrich fern is that it is the source of edible fiddleheads for gourmet spring meals.

Cultural Information: In the wild, *Matteuccia struthiopteris* grows in moist woods and swamps. Plant it in a similar rich, moist, shady spot in the garden. Space the individual ferns about 3 feet apart.
Uses: Groundcover for the woodland or shade garden, edible fiddleheads.

Osmunda (oz-MUN-dah) **cinnamon, interrupted and royal ferns, Easy.** ◐ ●

Origin: Eastern United States
Habitat: Swamps and moist woods
Zones: 3 to 10
Height: 3 to 4 feet
Characteristics: *Osmunda cinnamomea* (cinnamon fern) and *O. claytoniana* (interrupted fern) have very similar looking fronds. Both can reach a height of 4 feet in rich moist soil, but 3 feet is more likely. Cinnamon fern grows in swamps and moist woods and bears its spores in cinnamon stick–like inflorescences. The interrupted fern is found in moist to slightly drier sites and its brown spores occur halfway up the stems, "interrupting" the green leaves of its frond. Because the interrupted fern is adapted to drier conditions, it is often the more useful of the two in a garden setting that is not continually moist. Given a constantly moist site, the cinnamon fern would be the best choice because its uninterrupted green fronds are cleaner and more dramatic looking. The leaves of *Osmunda regalis* (the royal fern) are much more divided, giving it an airier appearance. This 3-foot fern grows in shady swamps and on hummocks of soil in full

Matteuccia struthiopteris

Osmunda cinnamomea

sun in bogs or lake edges. In the garden it is easily grown in any moist, fertile soil in partial shade. It is the beauty of the group, changing to a pure yellow in fall.
Cultural Information: Cinnamon fern requires a moist, rich shady site. Interrupted fern and royal fern will grow in similar conditions, but interrupted fern is also tolerant of drier shade gardens, while royal fern can even grow in full sun provided it is in a very wet site. Space these ferns about 2½ feet apart.
Uses: Shade and woodland gardens. Royal fern can also be

Polystichum acrostichoides

Polystichum (poe-LIS-ti-kum) **Christmas and sword ferns,** Easy. ◗ ●
Origin: Eastern and western United States
Habitat: Moist woods
Zones: 3 to 10
Height: 2 to 6 feet
Characteristics: Polystichum acrostichoides (Christmas fern) is a common evergreen fern found in forests of the eastern half of the United States. It reaches a height of about 2 feet and has a spread of equal size. The Christmas fern is hardy in Zones 3 to 10. *P. munitum* (western swordfern) is equally common in the Pacific Northwest where it carpets the forest floor. In cultivation this ever-green fern is usually 2 to 3 feet tall, but in the rain forests of the Olympic Peninsula it often grows to the magnificent height of 5 to 6 feet. The western swordfern performs best in the milder climates of Zones 6 to 8.
Cultural Information: Both of the polystichums are easy to grow in any rich, moist, partially shaded site. They should be spaced 2½ feet apart.
Uses: Woodland and shade gardens, evergreen groundcover.

Royal fern; see ***Osmunda regalis***

Wood fern; see ***Dryopteris***

grown in very moist sunny sites, such as along the banks of a pond.

Ostrich fern; see ***Matteuccia***

GRASSES

As far as I'm concerned, no type of plant is more important than grasses in any sunny garden. All of the wildflowers that evolved in sunny situations such as meadows or prairies will be found in nature to be growing in combination with grasses. The foliage of grasses provides a repetitious vertical line against which the blooms of wildflowers appear in harmonious accord. Even a quick observation of wild habitats will make you aware that in nature the ratio of grasses to flowers is always high. The moving and constantly changing grasses define a meadow or prairie, while the colored flowers merely provide an ephemeral sparkle.

I always design my sunny gardens with wild habitats in mind. First, I place the grasses that will provide the rhythm and continuity of planting. I then select the flowers. I have found that most of the taller native grasses do not stand up through the entire winter, so I often use them in combination with some of the sturdier nonnative grasses such as miscanthus and pennisetum, which do remain erect all winter long. I continue to use native grasses in all of my plantings because they have good fall color and a lighter, less formal habit of growth than the nonnative grasses. All the native grasses are best planted in spring, and the easiest method of propagation is by division, also in spring.

Andropogon (an-droe-POE-gone) **bluestem,** Easy. ○
Origin: Throughout the United States
Habitat: Meadows, fields and prairies
Zones: 3 to 9
Height: 2 to 7 feet
Characteristics: The bluestems are found growing throughout the United States. Big bluestem (*Andropogon gerardii*) plays a particularly important role in U.S. history and ecology, for it

Andropogon gerardii

was the dominant plant of the eastern tall grass prairies. Stories are told of it being so tall and so profuse that a man on horseback could be lost among its blades. In cultivation this grass has a basal mass of foliage about 2 to 3 feet tall, from which rise the flowering blades to a height of 6 to 7 feet. In late summer, the grass begins to change to a shimmering copper color, which lasts through the fall. Big bluestem needs full sun and average to dry soils. In a moist to average soil this grass may need staking or the support of nearby tall growing plants. Little bluestem (*A. scoparius,* or *Schizachyrium scoparium* as it is sometimes called) is a smaller and more refined version that reaches a height of only 2 to 3 feet. It prefers drier soils in full sun and turns a showy reddish copper in fall.

Cultural Information: Plant the bluestems in spring in average to dry soils in full sun. Space big bluestem plants 3 feet apart and little bluestems 18 inches apart.

Uses: Prairies, meadows, perennial borders, groundcover.

Bluestem; see ***Andropogon***

Bouteloua (boo-tuh-LOO-ah) **gramma grass,** Easy. ○
Origin: Throughout the United States
Habitat: Dry meadows and prairies
Zones: 4 to 9
Height: 12 to 18 inches
Characteristics: The gramma grasses were important components of the drier short grass

Bouteloua gracilis

prairies. These low-growing, 12- to 18-inch plants are an essential addition to all dry gardens and xeriscapes, although they are tolerant of soils of average moisture as well. *Bouteloua curtipendula* (side oats gramma grass) is native to the eastern two-thirds of the United States and has gray-green leaves with one-sided flowers in early summer. *B. gracilis* (blue gramma or mosquito grass) grows wild in the western half of the United States. It also has gray-green leaves, but its flowers are held at a 45° angle from the stem and look like combs. These inflorescences make wonderful dried flowers.

Cultural Information: Both gramma grasses should be planted in spring and grown in full sun in average to dry soils. Space the individual plants 12 to 18 inches apart.

Uses: Sunny perennial garden, dry meadow or prairie. Blue gramma grass makes a good dried flower.

Chasmanthium latifolium (chas-MAN-thee-um la-ti-FOE-lee-um) **wild oat grass,** Easy. ○ ◑
Origin: Eastern and central United States
Habitat: Rich woodlands and stream sides
Zones: 5 to 9
Height: 2 to 3 feet
Characteristics: Wild oat grass bears very ornamental, flat, oat-like seeds that change from a fresh green in summer to a lustrous gold in fall. The seeds remain on the grass for most of the winter unless you've cut them for use in dried flower arrangements. *Chasmanthium latifolium* grows to a height of 3 feet and is sometimes sold under its old name of *Uniola latifolia.*
Cultural Information: Wild oat grass prefers a moist, rich garden soil in light shade to full sun. Space plants 2 to 3 feet apart.
Uses: Perennial gardens in full sun or partial shade, dried flower arrangements.

Dropseed, prairie; see ***Sporobolus***

Chasmanthium latifolium

Panicum virgatum *'Haense Hermes'* with Aster umbellatus

Sorghastrum nutans
'Sioux Blue'

Sporobolus heterolepis

Gramma grass; see ***Bouteloua***

Indian grass; see ***Sorghastrum***

Oat grass, wild; see ***Chasmanthium***

Panicum virgatum (PAN-i-come vir-GAY-tum) **switchgrass,** Easy. ○ ◐
Origin: Eastern two-thirds of the United States
Habitat: Prairies, meadows and wood edges
Zones: 3 to 9
Height: 4 to 5 feet
Characteristics: Switchgrass can be found in prairies, meadows and wood edges from Nevada to the East. This 4- to 5-foot grass is extremely adaptable, growing in damp or dry soil in full sun. In late summer it produces many panicles of airy seedpods that provide good food for wildlife during the winter. The fall color of the species is golden, but several cultivars exist that turn a dramatic burgundy in late summer and hold that color through most of the fall. These cultivars are nearly identical with one another and go under the names of 'Haense Hermes', 'Rotstrahlbusch' and 'Rehbraun'. These forms were selected in Germany, where grasses are very much appreciated in perennial and shrub plantings. A newcomer on the scene is the cultivar 'Heavy Metal', the foliage of which has a strong bluish cast during the spring and summer.
Cultural Information: Switchgrass is easily grown in sun to light shade and in damp to dry soils. In shadier sites it might need some staking. Space plants 3 to 4 feet apart.
Uses: Perennial gardens, wildlife plantings and meadows and prairies.

Prairie dropseed; see ***Sporobolus***

Sorghastrum nutans (sore-GAS-trum NEW-tanz) **Indian grass,** Easy. ○
Origin: Throughout the United States
Habitat: Meadows and prairies
Zones: 3 to 9
Height: 5 to 6 feet
Characteristics: Indian grass is native throughout most of the United States. It was the second most important grass of the tall grass prairie, after big bluestem. Indian grass grows to a height of 5 to 6 feet. In late summer the plants produce showy copper flowers with prominent yellow pollen sacs. Soon after that, the entire plant turns a brilliant copper color for the fall. Indian grass makes a very graceful and natural addition to a garden setting. The foliage of the cultivar called 'Sioux Blue' is a good blue tone, which makes a nice contrast with other perennials during the summer months.
Cultural Information: Sorghastrum nutans prefers a rich, moist soil in full sun, although it is also tolerant of drier and less fertile conditions. Space plants 3 to 4 feet apart.
Uses: Perennial garden, meadows and prairies.

Sporobolus heterolepis (spah-ROB-ah-lus he-te-row-LEP-is) **prairie dropseed,** Easy. ○
Origin: Central United States
Habitat: Prairies and grasslands
Zones: 3 to 9
Height: 3 feet
Characteristics: Prairie dropseed is native to prairies and grasslands of the central United States. While not commonly grown, this refined plant is a tremendous addition to any garden. It has a 12-inch narrow-leafed tuft of basal foliage and in late summer bears light, airy seedpods that reach a height of 3 feet. As an added bonus, the foliage turns a bright golden orange in fall.
Cultural Information: To grow well, Sporobolus heterolepis requires only full sun and average to dry garden soil. Space plants 12 to 18 inches apart.
Uses: Perennial garden, meadows and prairies, groundcover.

Switchgrass; see ***Panicum***

Wild oat grass; see ***Chasmanthium***

PERENNIALS

Herbaceous perennials are plants that survive more than two years, yet do not form woody stems. The top growth of perennials dies down in winter, but the roots remain alive, and each spring new stems and leaves emerge from the ground. In flower gardens, perennials are grown for their ornamental characteristics such as colorful blossoms or interesting leaves.

This past decade or so has seen a phenomenal growth in the popularity of perennial plants. People like the idea of planting something that will flower for more than one year. Though perennials will not bloom all season long the way many annuals do, you can achieve a garden of constantly changing color and foliage textures by mixing and matching several types of perennials with staggered seasons of bloom.

Across the United States there is a great abundance and diversity of perennial wildflowers. Many are worthy of a place in the garden, while a few are too weedy looking or invasive to be used. Below is a selection of wildflowers that deserve a place in our gardens. Some are already well loved and commonly grown, while others are waiting to be discovered.

Allegheny spurge; see *Pachysandra*

Allium cernuum (AL-ee-um SIR-new-um) **nodding pink onion,** Easy. ○ ◑ 🌡
Origin: Throughout the United States

Habitat: Moist rocky meadows
Zones: 4 to 8
Height: 18 inches
Colors: Pale pink to deep lavender-pink
Characteristics: The nodding pink onion is found on moist, often rocky ground throughout the United States. It reaches a height of 18 inches, and its drooping pink flowers are a graceful addition to the early summer garden. *Allium cernuum* foliage is the typical green grasslike growth of all of the onion family and is lower than the flowers, about 10 inches tall.
Cultural Information: Allium cernuum is best planted in small groups in the garden, so the dainty 3-inch flowers may be seen *en masse.* The plants should be grown in sun to light shade in average to moist garden soil. Set the plants about 10 to 12 inches apart. The plants will form new bulblets next to the mother bulb, which makes each individual plant look lusher and bloom more fully every year. Unless you want to encourage self-sowing, it is a good idea to deadhead the flowers soon after bloom. Propagate this allium by division or give the seeds 2 months of cold, moist stratification.
Uses: Perennial border, groundcover under shrubs, rock garden, meadow or cut flower.

Alumroot; see *Heuchera*

American cowslip; see *Dodecatheon*

Allium cernuum

Amorpha canescens

Amorpha canescens (a-MOR-fa ka-NES-ens) **leadplant,** Moderate. ○ ◖ 🌸
Origin: Central United States
Habitat: Prairies
Zones: 2 to 8
Height: 3 to 4 feet
Colors: Deep blue-purple with orange anthers
Characteristics: Technically classified as a shrub, the leadplant behaves more like a perennial in its manner of growth. It is never a large plant, usually growing no more than 3 feet in height and about the

same or more in width. All season long it is graced with feathery gray-green leaves from which arise spikes of intense deep blue-purple flowers that are further enhanced by prominent orange anthers.

Cultural Information: Amorpha canescens grows best in sandy, drier soils in full sun. It is quite tolerant of soils with a high pH. A single plant is dramatic enough to stand on its own; many plants can be massed together for a low shrublike effect. Be aware that the leadplant is slow to mature and may take up to 3 years to attain its full size. Space the plants 3 feet apart. In the first few years you may want to fill in the extra space around the plant with annuals or an easily transplanted perennial that can be moved once the leadplant matures. Soak the seeds in hot water for 24 hours before sowing.

Uses: Perennial border, shrub border, dry meadow or prairie.

Amsonia (am-SON-ee-a) **blue dogbane, willow amsonia, blue star,** Easy. ○ ◑

Origin: Southeastern United States
Habitat: Sandy woodlands

Amsonia tabernaemontana

Zones: 5 to 9
Height: 2 to 4 feet
Colors: Light steel blue to sky blue
Characteristics: All of the amsonias make excellent low-maintenance perennials with lovely starlike blue flowers in spring and healthy, glossy green foliage that turns a beautiful clear yellow in autumn. The dense, rounded habit of growth and long, willowlike leaves make this plant a focal point in the garden. There are several species of amsonia that differ primarily by the shape of the leaf. *A. tabernaemontana* bears the typical willow-shaped leaf and grows to a height of 3 to 4 feet, while *A. tabernaemontana* var. *salicifolia* has narrower leaves. The leaves of *A. ciliata* are the narrowest of all, and this is a beautiful and refined accent to any planting. *A. montana* is a dwarf form, reaching only 2 feet with darker blue flowers than most amsonias.

Cultural Information: Amsonias are easy to grow in any sunny to partially shaded site that has average to moist soil. In full sun they should need no staking, while in part shade you can prune back the plant by one-third in late spring to encourage branching and to prevent it from flopping. Space the plants about 3 feet apart for the large-growing specimens and 2 feet apart for the lower-growing *A. montana.* Soak the seeds overnight in warm water before sowing and then be patient because germination can be slow. Plants may also be increased by division or late spring cuttings.

Uses: Perennial border, foundation plantings, transitional plant along lightly shaded woodland gardens and in shrub borders.

Anemone (a-NEM-oh-nee) **anemone,** Easy, Moderate or Difficult (depending on the species). ○ ◑

Origin: Throughout the United States
Habitat: Moist meadows and woodland edges
Zones: 3 to 8
Height: 6 inches to 2 feet
Colors: White, lavender
Characteristics: Native anemones vary from delicate, ephemeral 6-inch woodland flowers to the robust meadow-growing Canadian anemone to the exquisitely beautiful anemones that inhabit cooler but well-drained alpine regions. All anemones produce single, 5-petaled blossoms in the spring. *Anemone canadensis,* the Canadian anemone, which grows in moist meadows in the Northeast, is an aggressive colonizer, growing to a height of 18 inches to 2 feet. This mounding palmate-leafed plant is covered with white flowers during the months of May and June, making for a dramatic display. It is extremely easy to grow, spreading most happily in moist to average garden soil in full sun. Be forewarned: This plant can be extremely invasive and is best placed where a vigorous groundcovering plant is needed. One very good use for this plant is along the edge of a pond or stream where it may spread unchecked and provide a low edging that will not block a view. Other anemones such as *A. patens* (pasque flower) are

Anemone canadensis

more delicate beauties. This plant (the state flower of South Dakota) has white to lavender hairy flowers in May, which produce silvery plumed seed-pods in June. It prefers a well-drained sandy soil in full sun.
Cultural Information: Space the *Anemone canadensis* 3 feet apart and *A. patens* 1 foot apart. The Canadian anemone is most easily propagated by division in spring. The pasque flower can be grown from seed, which requires a period of moist, cold stratification in order to germinate.
Uses: Depending upon the species, meadow, pond side, groundcover, rock garden.

Aquilegia (ak-wi-LEE-jee-ah)
columbine, Easy. ○ ◑ ◖ ✿
Origin: Throughout the United States
Habitat: Woods and rocky slopes
Zones: 3 to 8
Height: 8 inches to 2 feet
Colors: Red, yellow, blue, white, lavender, pink
Characteristics: The long-spurred columbines have long been among the most beloved spring flowers. These beauties are the result of hybridizing several of the wild eastern and western species of columbines, such as the short-spurred red and yellow *Aquilegia canadensis* and *A. formosa,* with the long-spurred blue and white *A. caerulea* and yellow *A. chrysantha.* The hybrids come in a huge variety of colors and combinations and are sold under names such as the McKana hybrids and the Musik series.

Columbines are not long-lived in the garden, often last-ing only 3 to 5 years. They are, however, well worth replacing on a regular basis because their long and showy season of bloom make them an essential component of a spring garden. All of the species are easy to grow and worthy of cultivation. The short-spurred *A. canadensis* is a dainty but tough red and yellow 12-inch beauty that inhabits rocky woodlands throughout the East. The flowers look best in partial shade. Full sun will bleach the red to a paler, washed-out orange. Once established, this species will self-sow and happily naturalize itself about the garden. *A. formosa* looks like a taller version of *A. canadensis.* It grows to be 2 feet or taller and is found in similar rocky woodlands in the western half of the United States.
Cultural Information: The long-spurred columbines grow best in average to moist garden soil in full sun to light shade. The short-spurred *Aquilegia canadensis* and *A. formosa* look best in partial shade. These two species are also more tolerant of dry conditions than the long-spurred types. Columbines are easy to grow from seed sown in late spring or early summer. Expect flowers the following spring. Plant about 12 inches apart in the garden.
Uses: Perennial garden, rock garden, woodland garden and cut flower.

Aralia racemosa (ah-RAIL-yah ras-eh-MOSE-ah) **spikenard,** Easy. ◑ ●
Origin: Most of the United States
Habitat: Rich, moist woods

Aquilegia *'McKana Hybrids'*

Zones: 4 to 8
Height: 3 to 5 feet
Colors: White with deep purple berries in fall
Characteristics: Spikenard is a great bold-foliaged plant with elongated panicles of white flowers in spring and lustrous dark purple berries in the fall. *Aralia racemosa* makes a dramatic addition to any shade garden or woodland planting, reaching a height of 5 feet with an equal spread in width.
Cultural Information: Spikenard is easily grown in a rich, moisture-retentive soil in partial shade. Set plants about 4 feet apart to give them room to fully mature. Cut back the spent stems in late fall. To grow from seed, collect the berries when ripe and rub off pulp in a sieve, washing away the pulp with running water. Sow the seeds immediately in the fall and allow the seeds a period of moist, cold stratification outdoors. Seeds will germinate the following spring and plants should flower when 2 years old.
Uses: Bold textural plant for the shade garden and woodland walk.

Aralia racemosa

Arctostaphylos uva-ursi

Arisaema triphyllum

Artemisia ludoviciana
'Silver King'

Arctostaphylos uva-ursi

(ark-toe-STAFF-i-los oo-vah-ER-see) **bearberry,** Moderate. ○ ◑ ❋
Origin: Throughout northern two-thirds of the United States
Habitat: Dry sandy or rocky soil
Zones: 2 to 7
Height: 4 inches
Color: White
Characteristics: Bearberry is a low evergreen groundcover that sends out long runners and can quickly cover difficult exposed and dry sites. It has innocuous white flowers in spring that form red berries in late summer and fall. The glossy, dark green leaves make it a very ornamental groundcover.
Cultural Information: Due to its widely spreading root system, bearberry is difficult to transplant. It is wisest to plant container-grown stock in a sunny, sandy, well-drained site. Although the plant is extremely drought-tolerant when established, the new plants will need to be watered well throughout the first growing season to encourage the roots to spread in the dense and deep manner that they grow in the wild. To propagate, take cuttings of the side shoots, not the long runners, in early winter or late spring. Be patient, because it may take a while for the roots to form. Transplant newly rooted cuttings gently.
Uses: Evergreen groundcover, dune stabilizer.

Arisaema triphyllum

(ar-i-SEE-mah try-FY-lum) **jack-in-the-pulpit,** Easy. ◑ ●
Origin: Eastern half of the United States
Habitat: Rich, moist woodlands
Zones: 4 to 9
Height: 6 inches to 3 feet
Colors: Brown and green striped intriguing blossoms
Characteristics: The "jack" is a beloved wildflower of the early spring garden. Its curved brown and green striped spathe with its fingerlike green spadix inside never fails to enchant young and old alike. The root of the arisaema is actually a corm that looks like a flat-bottomed turnip. When mature, the plant will produce a very ornamental cluster of ripe red berries in the fall.
Cultural Information: Jack-in-the-pulpits are easily grown in any light, moderately moist soil in partial shade. Growing the really big jacks can become something of an obsession similar to that of growing great pumpkins. I have found that a light soil (which permits easy growth of the corm) and plenty of moisture are the keys to large plants. It is best to move jacks in the fall just before the plant goes dormant. When happy with its site it should self-sow freely, providing you with many babies for future gardens.
Uses: Shade and woodland gardens.

Artemisia ludoviciana

(are-teh-MEE-zee-ah loo-do-vik-EE-aye-na) **white sage,** Easy. ○ ◑ ❋
Origin: Western half of the United States
Habitat: Prairies and sandy dry sites
Zones: 3 to 9
Height: 2 to 4 feet
Colors: Silvery foliage, small whitish flowers
Characteristics: White sage is a wonderful plant against which to contrast and highlight other flowers. The aromatic, jaggedly cut silver foliage also makes a

terrific dried flower and is often used as the basis of dried flower wreaths. Several cultivars exist, such as 'Silver King', which is more compact than the species, growing about 2½ to 3 feet tall, and 'Silver Queen', which has deeply cut leaves.

Cultural Information: White sage is easily grown in any sunny garden with average to dry soil. Be aware that the plant spreads by creeping roots and can become invasive in a small garden. It is not, however, too hard to pull out and is definitely worth including in the garden for its silvery foliage. Division is the easiest way to obtain more plants.

Uses: Sunny perennial garden, dried flower.

Aruncus dioicus (a-RUN-kiss dye-OH-i-kiss) **goat's beard,** Easy. ◑ ●

Origin: Northern North America
Habitat: Rich woodlands
Zones: 3 to 7
Height: 4 to 6 feet
Color: White
Characteristics: Goat's beard looks like a giant astilbe. A mature specimen reaches a height of 6 feet and has an equal breadth. It bears large, white, plumelike inflorescences in late spring. The bold foliage and great size of this plant make it useful as a backdrop for the shade garden and to provide mass and bulk in a design.
Cultural Information: Aruncus is easily grown in partial shade and rich, moist soil. In too much shade or too dry a site, the plant will not flower well

or reach its normal great size. Space the plants about 4 feet apart and water well until established. Division is the best way to increase the number of plants.

Uses: Shade or woodland garden, massing, providing a backdrop or screen.

Asarum (a-SAR-um) **wild ginger,** Easy. ◑ ●

Origin: Most of the United States
Habitat: Rich woodlands
Zones: 4 to 8
Height: 8 to 12 inches
Color: Grown for ornamental green leaves
Characteristics: The wild gingers occur in rich woodlands throughout the United States in both deciduous and evergreen forms. Some botanists have lumped the evergreen forms into the genus *Hexastylis*. All gingers bear dark red flowers under their foliage, which are not generally noticeable. *Asarum canadense* (deciduous wild ginger) has heart-shaped, gray-green leaves that quickly spread to form a dense groundcover. It is native to the eastern United States. *A. arifolium* and *A. shuttleworthii* are both evergreen species native to the Southeast and hardy to Zone 6. They differ in the shape of their leaves. *A. arifolium* has arrow-shaped leaves while *A. shuttleworthii* has more rounded leaves. *A. hartwegii* and *A. caudatum* are western evergreen gingers. Both of these have rounded leaves as well.
Cultural Information: The evergreen gingers are clump formers and should be used as accent plants in the shade gar-

Aruncus dioicus

Asarum virginicum

den. Their shiny, sometimes gray, mottled foliage provides a quiet contrast in a planting. *A. canadense* can be massed and planted with 1 foot between plants. It will quickly form a dense groundcover, even in fairly dark corners. For fastest growth, plant in a moist to average garden soil. Division is the best way to increase all of the gingers.

Uses: Shade or woodland garden, groundcover.

Asclepias tuberosa

Asclepias *(seedpod)*

Aster novae-angliae

Asclepias (ass-CLAY-pee-us) **milkweed, butterfly weed,** Easy. ○ 🛈

Origin: Throughout the United States

Habitat: Sunny fields and meadows

Zones: 4 to 9

Height: 2 to 4 feet

Colors: Orange, yellow, pink

Characteristics: All members of the milkweed genus bear a characteristic seedpod with cottonlike threads attached to the seed inside. These seedpods are often collected for use in dried flower arrangements. The milkweeds also have a milky sap that can be seen if a leaf or stem is snapped. The showiest of the milkweeds is *Asclepias tuberosa* (butterfly weed). It bears waxy, flat-topped orange flowers in July at a height of about 2 feet. The shade of orange varies considerably from yellowish to reddish. One seed mixture called 'Gay Butterflies' has emphasized some of these red and yellow forms. *A. incarnata* (swamp or showy milkweed) is found in moist meadows in the East and has dusty pink flowers on 4-foot plants.

Cultural Information: The butterfly weed is a long-lived perennial with a deep taproot that resents transplanting. It is happiest when sited in a sunny, dry, sandy location. Butterfly weed is one of those perennials that is slow to come up in spring, so be careful when digging in the garden early in the season. The bright orange flowers look nice intermingled with other warm-toned summer flowers such as rudbeckias. They also contrast well with blue flowers such as platycodon. Swamp milkweed prefers a moist rich soil in sun. Space both species approximately 2 feet apart. Milkweed seed quickly loses viability, so it is best sown soon after collecting. I have found that a greater percentage of seeds germinate when given a period of moist, cold stratification than when left untreated. Seedlings take several years to reach maturity.

Uses: Sunny perennial garden, meadow, cut flower, dried flower (for the seedpods).

Aster (ASS-ter) **aster,** Easy. ○ ◑ 🛈

Origin: Throughout the United States

Habitat: Meadows and prairies, wood edges

Zones: 4 to 8

Height: 1 to 5 feet

Colors: White, pink, lavender, blue

Characteristics: The many native asters come into their glory in the late summer and fall. Smothered with finely rayed flowers that have bright yellow centers, asters put on a spectacular show of color at heights ranging from 12 inches to 5 feet. Asters can be found in almost any habitat including woodland edges, sandy beaches, moist meadows, alpine areas and the driest of prairies. No matter where you garden, there is an aster for you. Perhaps the best known asters are the various cultivars of the New England and New York asters, *Aster novi belgii* and *A. novae-angliae.* The species form of each of these has deep violet flowers, grows to a height of about 4 feet and is found in moist places along the East Coast. Colors of the cultivars range from the white of 'Mt. Everest' to the clear pink of 'Harrington's Pink' and from the shocking bright rose of 'Alma Potschke' to the pale lavender blue of the dwarf 'Prof. Kippenburg'.

A. lateriflorus horizontalis is quite a different beast. It has many tiny white flowers highlighted by bronze foliage. It grows in a distinctive horizontal fashion at a height of only about 18 inches. Often overlooked because the blossoms are not showy, the plant is wonderful weaving in among other perennials in the garden or as a groundcover. You will find that it is tolerant of poor dry soils and sun to partial shade. There are other dainty-flowered aster species, often called heath asters, that serve a similar function in a garden. *A. ericoides* 'Esther' is a pale pink form while *A. pringeli* 'Monte Casino' bears a profusion of medium-sized white daisies.

A. umbellatus is a beauty that deserves a more exciting common name than flat-topped white aster. It grows to a height of 5 feet and is covered by small white blossoms with a yellow center, giving the whole plant a very pale yellow appearance in late August through September.

A. spectabilis (showy aster), which reaches a height of only 18 inches, has extremely large blue flowers with golden centers. It inhabits sandy dry areas and thus is a useful perennial for the dry sunny garden.

Cultural Information: Most of the native asters are tolerant of average garden soil in full sun. Depending upon their habitat of origin some can also be grown in moister soils, such as the New England and New York asters as well as the flat-topped asters. Others such as the showy aster and the heath asters are useful in dry soils. If you wish to avoid staking the taller aster species, you can cut them back by about one-third of their height in early June, which will cause them to branch and flower at a lower height. I learned the hard way that it's important to cut back before a rain. One year I cut back my asters in June and then it didn't rain all summer long. I was left with mowed-looking asters all season. Normally a little rain or irrigation will spur the plant into growth, thus hiding the cuts within a week.

Space asters anywhere from 18 inches apart for the dwarfer growing types to 3 feet apart for the taller growing species. Seeds germinate after a period of moist, cold stratification. Plants can also be divided.

Many of the asters make showy cut flowers for bouquets. In fact, I used the pink and lavender tones of the New England asters as the theme for my September wedding. The trick is to cut the flowers 36 to 48 hours before they are to be viewed. The flowers close up in shock soon after being cut and it takes them a day or so in water to reopen.

Uses: Perennial borders, cut flower, naturalizing.

Baptisia (bap-TEE-zee-ah) wild indigo, Easy. ○ ◑ ✳ ▮

Origin: Eastern half of the United States
Habitat: Meadows, prairies, thickets
Zones: 3 to 9
Height: 3 to 5 feet
Colors: Blue, white and yellow
Characteristics: Baptisias are handsome garden plants with gray-green foliage and large, 10- to 12-inch-long flower spikes reminiscent of a lupine. They are long lived and very easy to grow. When not in bloom, their bold foliage and bushlike habit of growth pro-

Baptisia australis

vide structure to any planting and a foil to the later blooms of other perennials. In autumn, the large inflated seedpods turn a dark brown and are ornamental enough to warrant inclusion in dried flower arrangements and wreaths. *Baptisia australis* (wild blue indigo) is the best known of the wild indigo species. It forms a 5-foot bushlike perennial and produces great quantities of blue flowers in spring. *B. leucantha* reaches 5 feet as well, but it has white blossoms in spring. The smaller *B. pendula* (sometimes called *B. lactea*) grows to 2½ to 3 feet. It has white flowers highlighted by dark purple stems. *B. tinctoria* (yellow wild indigo) inhabits dry, sterile sites in the wild. It produces many small clusters of yellow pealike flowers in midsummer over a rounded 3-foot bush. While not as showy as its blue and white flowered cousins, this plant has a more delicate beauty that earns it a place in any dry, sunny garden.

Cultural Information: It is easiest to transplant baptisias while they are young, because older plants form deep taproots that make digging difficult. Most baptisias prefer a rich, fertile soil in sun to light shade. *B. tinctoria* grows best in drier, sandier sites in full sun. Space the plants 3 feet apart. The seeds germinate well after soaking in warm water for 24 hours. *Uses:* Perennial border, shrub border, cutting, dried arrangements (the seedpods).

Barren strawberry; see *Waldsteinia*

Bearberry; see *Arctostaphylos*

Beard-tongue; see *Penstemon*

Beebalm; see *Monarda*

Bellwort; see *Uvularia*

Black-eyed Susan; see *Rudbeckia*

Black snakeroot; see *Cimicifuga*

Blanket flower; see *Gaillardia*

Blazing star; see *Liatris*

Bleeding-heart, wild; see *Dicentra*

Bloodroot; see *Sanguinaria*

Bluebells, Virginia; see *Mertensia*

Blue dogbane; see *Amsonia*

Blue star; see *Amsonia*

Boltonia asteroides 'Snowbank'

Boltonia asteroides

(bowl-TONE-ee-ah ass-ter-OI-deez)
boltonia, Easy. ○ 🔋 🏵
Origin: Eastern two-thirds of the United States
Habitat: Moist meadows
Zones: 4 to 9
Height: 3 to 6 feet
Colors: White, lavender, pink
Characteristics: The species *Boltonia asteroides* is a coarse, tall plant. The dwarf form known as 'Snowbank', however, is a commonly grown perennial that reaches a height of only 3 to 4 feet. It has gray-green foliage and in August and September features many small white daisy flowers with yellow centers. The ease of growth, long flowering period and gray foliage have earned 'Snowbank' a loyal following. 'Pink Beauty' is another variety that bears many clear pink flowers in the autumn. It is taller and often requires staking. *B. latisquama* var. *nana* bears large inflorescences of lavender flowers on a 3-foot plant.
Cultural Information: Boltonias prefer an average to moist garden site in sun. They can be grown in partial shade but then may require staking. Space the 3-foot varieties about 18 inches apart, and the taller growing forms about 2½ feet apart. Seeds germinate well after a period of moist, cold stratification, however, seeds of the cultivars may revert to the habit or color of the species. The cultivars are best perpetuated by late spring or early summer cuttings.
Uses: Perennial garden, naturalizing, cut flower.

Bowman's root; see *Porteranthus*

Bugbane; see *Cimicifuga*

Bunchberry; see *Cornus*

Burnet, Canadian; see *Sanguisorba*

Butterfly weed; see *Asclepias*

California fuchsia; see *Zauschneria*

Callirhoe involucrata

(kal-LI-ro-ee   in-vol-you-CRATE-ah)
wine cups or poppy mallow,
Easy. ○ ◗ ✳ ✿
Origin: Central plains states
Habitat: Prairies
Zones: 3 to 9
Height: 1 foot
Color: Magenta-rose
Characteristics: Callirhoe is a sprawling, sun-loving member of the mallow family. It sends out procumbent 3-foot stems that bear vivid rose-purple cups all summer long. The poppy mallow has a deep taproot that enables it to grow in very dry soil. This plant may be used as a long-blooming groundcover in very harsh sites or it can be permitted to wind its long stems around the base of other plants in the perennial garden.
Cultural Information: Space plants about 2 feet apart or place them closer when combining with other flowers, since the stems will weave themselves around the other plants without smothering them. Water all newly planted plants well for the first season until the roots are well established. Poppy mallow may be propagated by seed, which requires several months of moist, cold stratification before it germinates.
Uses: Perennial garden, groundcover, meadows, xeriscapes.

Camass lily; see *Camassia*

Camassia

(ka-MA-see-ah)
camass lily, Easy. ○ ◗
Origin: North America, most common in Pacific Northwest
Habitat: Moist meadows
Zones: 4 to 8
Height: 2 to 3 feet

Colors: Blue, white
Characteristics: The starchy bulb of the camassia was a mainstay in the diet of the Indians of the Pacific Northwest where this flower is most common. Camassia has showy 2- to 3-foot spikes of blue to white star-shaped blossoms in May or June. Several species are available from bulb catalogs in the fall. The most common are *Camassia esculenta* (or *C. quamash*), which reaches a height of about 2 feet, and with flowers ranging in color from deep to pale blue, and the larger *C. cusickii*, which bears 3-foot-tall pale blue flowers. *C. cusickii* is the hardiest of all the species and can even survive in Zone 2 with protection. All camassias make beautiful additions to perennial borders and wild gardens.
Cultural Information: Plant camassia bulbs in the fall about 4 inches deep and 9 inches apart. They prefer rich, moist soil in full sun to light shade and look best when arranged in groups. Camassias are easy to grow and long lived. They will slowly multiply in the ground by offsets that can be divided. They can also be grown from seed but it often takes 4 years until they flower. Probably the best way to increase your collection is to purchase additional bulbs every fall.
Uses: Perennial garden, wild garden, meadow.

Canadian   burnet;   see *Sanguisorba*

Cardinal   flower;   see *Lobelia*

Callirhoe involucrata (*growing through leaves of* Alchemilla mollis)

Camassia cusickii

Cassia

(KAS-see-ah)   **wild senna,** Easy. ○ ◑ ◗ ✳
Origin: Eastern United States
Habitat: Dry thickets
Zones: 3 to 10
Height: 4 feet
Color: Yellow
Characteristics: Cassia forms a great mound of feathery leaves and showy yellow flowers in July, which are followed by ornamental beanlike seedpods. The leaves of the cassia also turn a showy, clear yellow in fall, adding to its 3-season beauty. Two species are commonly grown: *C. marilandica* and *C. hebecarpa*. To all but a

Cassia marilandica

taxonomic botanist, the two species are virtually identical and interchangeable in the garden.

Cultural Information: Wild senna prefers an average garden soil in full sun, but will grow in part shade or in dry conditions. It is very adaptable and easy to grow. Space the plants about 3 feet apart. Cassias can be grown from seed that should be soaked for 24 hours in warm water before sowing.

Uses: Perennial garden, meadow, shrub border, dried flower arrangements (the seedpods).

Celandine poppy; see *Stylophorum*

Chelone lyonii *with* Aster punicens

Chrysogonum virginianum

Chelone (che-LOW-nee) **turtle-head,** Easy. ○ ◑ ▮

Origin: Eastern United States
Habitat: Damp meadows and wood edges
Zones: 3 to 8
Height: 2 to 3 feet
Colors: White, pink
Characteristics: Chelone makes a pretty addition to the fall garden with its intriguing pink or white flowers held above shiny green leaves. With some imagination the beaked flowers are reminiscent of a turtle's head, hence its common name. *C. glabra* is the northernmost species, which bears white flowers touched with purple at the tips. *C. lyonii* is a more southern species that bears rose-pink flowers in fall. The similar *C. obliqua* has more purple-pink blossoms. Both of the pink-flowered turtleheads are showier garden plants than the white species.

Cultural Information: Chelones are easily grown in full sun to light shade in rich, moist soil. Space the plants about 2 feet apart because in time they will grow into a nice colony. Plants can be increased by division in spring or by seed. Seeds require several months of moist, cold stratification in order to germinate.

Uses: Perennial garden, wild garden, bog or waterside planting.

Chrysogonum virginianum (kris-OG-oh-num vir-jin-ee-AYE-num) **green and gold,** Easy. ◑ ● ❀

Origin: Southeastern United States
Habitat: Woods
Zones: 5 to 9

Height: 4 to 6 inches
Color: Golden yellow
Characteristics: Chrysogonum is a perky, long-blooming ground-cover for shady areas. The low creeping plants are covered with single yellow, marigoldlike flowers in spring, and they sporadically produce blossoms all summer and fall. Two varieties are commonly offered for sale. *Chrysogonum virginianum* var. *virgianum* has slightly larger flowers and may reach 8 inches, while the var. *australe* is a little shorter with somewhat smaller flowers but is a faster-growing groundcover.

Cultural Information: Plant chrysogonum in shady locations that remain fairly moist all season. The farther south it is grown, the more shade it will require. In very warm climates the flowering may cease for a while during the heat of the summer. In colder climates it is wise to protect the plants with a light mulch during the winter. Space plants about 10 inches apart. The best method of increasing plants is by division in spring or fall.

Uses: Groundcover, shade garden.

Chrysopsis villosa (kris-OP-sis vill-OH-sah) **hairy gold-aster,** Easy. ○ ◌ ✳ ▮ ❁

Origin: Western United States
Habitat: Dry prairies and meadows
Zones: 4 to 10
Height: 3 to 5 feet
Color: Golden yellow
Characteristics: The goldaster provides a cheery and welcome flush of yellow, daisylike flowers in late August through October. Its hairy, gray-green

leaves are a nice (but not dramatic) contrast to the typical wide green leaf of many of the fall blooming asters and sunflowers. *Chrysopsis villosa* is found in the wild from Wisconsin to Texas to California. This extremely adaptable plant grows equally well in average garden soil or in extremely dry sites.

Cultural Information: Space the plants about 2 feet apart in a sunny location. Make sure you water them well for the first season until the plants have developed a sufficiently wide-spreading system of roots to carry it through periods of drought. Plants may be grown from seed, which requires a period of moist, cold stratification in order to germinate.

Uses: Perennial garden, xeriscape, meadow or prairie.

Cimicifuga racemosa

(sim-i-si-FYOU-gah ray-se-MOE-sah)
bugbane, fairy candles, black snakeroot, Moderate.
◑ ●

Origin: Eastern United States
Habitat: Rich woods
Zones: 3 to 8
Height: 6 to 8 feet
Color: White
Characteristics: Cimicifuga racemosa makes a dramatic addition to any shady planting with its great pitchforklike inflorescences of white flowers that reach a towering height of 6 to 8 feet. Before the bugbane flowers appear, its 3-foot-tall astilbelike leaves provide a good foliage contrast in the garden, and after blossoming its rounded seedpods are ornamental as well.

Cultural Information: Cimici-

fuga prefers a rich, slightly moist soil in a partially shaded site. In shadier sites the flower stems may need staking. It looks best when planted in groups; set individual plants about 2½ feet apart. Cimicifuga is difficult to grow from seed, often requiring 2 to 3 years and lots of patience to germinate.

Uses: Shade garden, woodland plantings.

Columbine; see *Aquilegia*

Compass plant; see *Silphium*

Coneflower; see *Rudbeckia*

Coneflower, prairie; see *Ratibida*

Coneflower, purple; see *Echinacea*

Coral bells; see *Heuchera*

Coreopsis (kore-ee-OP-sis)
coreopsis, tickseed, Easy.
○ ✳ 🛈 ❀

Origin: Eastern United States and central plains states
Habitat: Dry meadows
Zones: 3 to 9
Height: 1 to 3 feet
Colors: Yellow, pink
Characteristics: The genus *Coreopsis* contains several great garden performers. Most have bright yellow flowers and are in bloom all summer long. *Coreopsis grandiflora* and *C. lanceolata* look very similar and have showy golden yellow flowers on leafy 2-foot plants. If you deadhead these plants you can have flowers for many months. There

Cimicifuga racemosa

Coreopsis verticillata '*Moonbeam*'

are single, semidouble and double-flowered varieties available. *C. verticillata* has become a mainstay of the perennial border in the 1980s and 1990s. The narrow, whorled leaves form a low mound of 1 to 1½ feet and the plant is covered with flowers during the summer. '*Moonbeam*' is an extremely popular cultivar. Its flowers are a beautiful shade of lemony yellow with a slight greenish cast that combines well with many other perennials. The spent blossoms of *C.*

verticillata can be sheared back once it has finished flowering to encourage a second period of bloom in fall. *C. auriculata nana* bears single orange-yellow flowers on creeping 6-inch plants. It flowers from late spring through fall and makes a good groundcover in a sunny site. *C. rosea* looks like a daintier version of *C. verticillata*, bearing many small pink flowers above its 1-foot foliage. Unlike other coreopsis, this species prefers a moist site.

Cultural Information: Coreopsis are extremely adaptable. They grow in average to dry garden soil in full sun. *Coreopsis rosea* is the exception to the rule,

Cornus canadensis

Dicentra *'Luxuriant'*

preferring a moister site. Plants should be spaced about 18 inches apart except for the dwarfer *C. auriculata nana*, which is best placed 12 inches apart. *C. grandiflora* and *C. lanceolata* last only about 2 to 3 years, but they will self-sow and are also easy to raise from seed. The easiest way to increase *C. verticillata*, *C. auriculata nana* or *C. rosea* is by division in spring or fall.

Uses: Perennial garden, meadow, cut flower.

Cornus canadensis (CORN-us can-ah-DEN-sis) **bunchberry,** Moderate. ◖ ● ✳

Origin: Northern North America
Habitat: Cool forests
Zones: 2 to 5
Height: 6 to 8 inches
Color: White
Characteristics: Cornus canadensis is the only perennial member of the dogwood family; all the other species are shrubs or trees. Forming a vigorous groundcover of low, whorled green leaves, it flowers in May or June with a familiar single white dogwood flower. In fall the seed of the bunchberry ripens to a showy red berry. With the white flowers in spring, attractive foliage in summer and red fruit in autumn, *C. canadensis* makes a beautiful groundcover for the woodland garden.

Cultural Information: Bunchberry grows best in a cool, moist, shaded garden. In such a site it is a moderately fast growing groundcover. The plants cannot tolerate warmer gardens for long and will soon disappear. Plants may be spaced anywhere from 4 to 12 inches apart depending on how quickly you

wish a dense groundcover to form. Water well for the first season. Division in spring is the fastest way to obtain more plants.

Uses: Groundcover, woodland or shade garden.

Cowslip, American; see *Dodecatheon*

Creeping valerian; see *Polemonium*

Culver's-root; see *Veronicastruon*

Cup-plant; see *Silphium*

Dicentra (die-SEN-trah) **wild bleeding-heart,** Easy. ◖ ▮ ✿

Origin: North America
Habitat: Woods
Zones: 3 to 9
Height: 8 to 18 inches
Colors: Pink, white
Characteristics: One of the most beloved spring flowers is the large bleeding-heart, *Dicentra spectabilis*, which comes from Europe. North America, however, has several lovely members of this genus that make very ornamental additions to the shaded garden. The most useful of the native bleeding-hearts are the 18-inch *D. eximia* from the East and the similar *D. formosa* from the West Coast. Both have ferny gray-green foliage and pink, narrowly heart-shaped flowers that begin blooming in spring and continue to blossom sporadically all summer and fall. There is a dainty white form of *D. eximia*, known as variety *alba*, which adds an air of refinement to the woodland garden. Oddly enough, American

wild bleeding-hearts have aroused more interest in Europe than they have here. Recently many beautiful hybrids and selections of the eastern and western species have been introduced, such as 'Luxuriant', with rose-pink flowers and slightly bluer foliage, and 'Snowdrift', which is a more vigorous white flowered selection. *D. cucullaria* is a smaller 8-inch plant that inhabits dry, rocky woodlands in the eastern half of the United States. It has adapted to its shady, dry situation by growing, flowering and setting seed early in the spring while there is still moisture in the ground from the spring rains and plenty of light shining down through the leafless trees above. By late spring the plants are completely dormant. The white flowers of *D. cucullaria* bear a strong resemblance to pants hanging on the clothesline, and because of this the plant was given the common name of dutchman's breeches many years ago.

Cultural Information: All of the dicentras grow best in average to moist shady sites; however, they are very adaptable and will tolerate drier conditions in more shade or sunnier exposures where there is moisture available. The species forms of *Dicentra eximia* and *D. formosa* will seed themselves about freely in the garden. The easiest way to obtain new plants is to dig and move the young seedlings. The white-flowered cultivars and the showy hybrids must be increased by division or tissue culture. Dutchman's breeches can be propagated by digging up the tiny lilylike

corms after the plant has gone dormant and then separating them into many smaller ones. Replant in the soil several inches deep and water. Next spring you will see foliage and the following year there will be flowers. Space the larger-growing wild bleeding-hearts 18 inches apart and the dutchman's breeches in drifts within several inches of one another.
Uses: Shade garden, woodlands, naturalizing.

Dodecatheon (doe-de-KATH-ee-on) **shooting star, American cowslip,** Moderate to Difficult. ○ ◐

Origin: North America
Habitat: Moist meadows and prairies
Zones: 4 to 8
Height: 1 to 2 feet
Colors: Pink, white
Characteristics: With their downward pointing, rocketlike nose and sharply reflexed petals, the dodecatheons are arguably the showiest of the American wildflowers. The blossoms arise from a basal rosette of fleshy leaves and are somewhat reminiscent of cyclamen blooms. After flowering, the shooting stars produce seed and then go dormant. There are several dozen species of shooting stars native to the United States, but two of the most commonly available are *Dodecatheon meadia* (native to eastern moist meadows) and *D. hendersonii* (native to western moist meadows). They are fairly similar and equally beautiful, although *D. hendersonii* has slightly larger basal leaves. A white form of *D. meadia* can be found as well.

Dodecatheon hendersonii

Cultural Information: Shooting stars grow in moist meadows in the wild and they need a similar moist, sunny site in the garden. Once the plants go dormant in midsummer they can withstand drier conditions. Dodecatheon are most dramatic when grown in groups, and the plants should be spaced about 12 inches apart. Plants may be grown from seed, which requires a period of moist, cold stratification for germination. It is best to sow the seeds in individual containers because they don't transplant well when young. In midsummer each year the seedlings will go dormant; don't worry, they haven't died. If you don't allow the pots to dry out completely following dormancy, you will see the plants come up again the following spring. It will take at least 3 seasons to produce flowers.
Uses: Rock garden, damp garden, meadow.

Echinacea purpurea *'White Swan'*

and move them to their new home once they are several inches tall. Water well for the first season. The seed cone of the purple coneflowers is extremely ornamental all winter long in the garden and is useful in dried flower arrangements.
Uses: Perennial garden, meadows, dried flower.

Eryngium yuccifolium
(e-RIN-gee-um YUCK-i-fole-ee-um) **rattlesnake master,** Easy. ○ ▮ ❀
Origin: Eastern and central United States
Habitat: Meadows and prairies
Zones: 3 to 10
Height: 4 to 6 feet
Color: White
Characteristics: This native eryngium has dramatic, 3-foot-high gray-green, bristle-edged leaves. It bears clustered balls of white flowers on 4- to 6-foot stems in midsummer. Although its leaves are reminiscent of a yucca, rattlesnake master prefers a moister habitat than does the drought-tolerant yucca. This plant is deciduous in cold climates and evergreen where it is warmer. The eryngium's linear

Echinacea (ek-in-AYE-see-ah) **purple coneflower,** Easy. ○ ✳ ▮ ❀
Origin: North America
Habitat: Meadows
Zones: 3 to 8
Height: 3 to 4 feet
Colors: Purple-pink, cream, yellow
Characteristics: Purple coneflower is a deservedly popular summer blooming wildflower. Showy pink petals with the contrasting orange-brown cone, a long period of bloom and ease of cultivation combine to make this plant a mainstay of the sunny summer garden. The plants are robust growers and are tolerant of both heat and cold. The most commonly grown species is *Echinacea purpurea*. Growers have also selected for pinker forms, cream-flowered forms and some whose petals don't droop as much as the species. Cultivars include 'Bright Star', 'Magnus' and 'White Swan'. The southeastern *E. pallida* has narrower petals that droop more, making

for a graceful appearance. *E. paradoxa* is a less well known species from Arkansas and Missouri that has orange-yellow rays.
Cultural Information: All echinaceas are easily grown in full sun in average to slightly dry garden soil. Plants tend to be taller than they are wide, and should be spaced about 2½ feet apart. The easiest way to obtain more plants is to watch for seedlings around the base of the mother plant in spring

Eryngium yuccifolium

gray leaves make an unusual and useful contrast to other perennials that prefer a similar moist to average garden soil. The common name of rattlesnake master refers to Indians' use of the root as a poultice for snakebites.

Cultural Information: Eryngium yuccifolium looks its best and is most upright in full sun, although it will grow in partial shade. It prefers a rich moist to average soil. The plants should be spaced 2 feet apart. Plants may be increased by division in the spring or by seed, which requires a period of moist, cold stratification in order to germinate.

Uses: Perennial garden, damp garden, meadow or prairie planting, cut flower.

Eupatorium (you-pah-TOR-ee-um) **Joe Pye weed, hardy ageratum, snakeroot,** Easy. ○ ◑ 🌡 ❀

Origin: Eastern and central North America
Habitat: Damp meadows and wood edges
Zones: 4 to 9
Height: 2 to 7 feet
Colors: White, pink, blue
Characteristics: The genus *Eupatorium* contains many garden-worthy members; the giants of the bunch are the Joe Pye weeds. With their great height, dusty rose flowers in late summer and architectural whorled leaves it is no wonder they are a common component of European gardens. Strangely, they are remarkably unappreciated in their native United States. The lore behind the common name is that Joe Pye was an Indian medicine man who is said to have used this plant in many of his cures. *E. purpureum, E. fistulosum* and *E. maculatum* are very similar and all are called Joe Pye weeds. Selected varieties include 'Atropurpureum', which has deeper purple stems, and 'Gateway', which is slightly dwarfer than most, reaching only 5 feet. Grown more often in American gardens is the blue *E. coelestinum*. This plant so resembles a late-blooming, 2- to 3-foot ageratum that it has been given the common name of hardy ageratum. It is hardy from Zones 6 to 10. Although it is beautiful, it should be placed with some care because it is a rapid spreader. *E. rugosum* (snakeroot) bears many flat-topped clusters of white flowers in early fall. It, too, is a vigorous grower and makes a lovely groundcover when planted with the equally competitive hardy ageratum. Snakeroot is a beautiful cut flower and has been described as baby's breath for fall.

Cultural Information: Joe Pye weeds prefer moist to average garden soil in full sun. *Eupatorium coelestinum* grows in full sun to light shade, while *E. rugosum* can grow in light to fairly dense shade. Both species tolerate moist to dry soils. All of the eupatoriums are extremely easy and satisfying to grow. Since all grow rapidly, they can be spaced a fair distance apart, up to 3 feet depending upon how fast you wish them to fill in. Plants can be divided in spring or can be grown from seed, which requires a period of moist, cold stratification in order to germinate.

Eupatorium maculatum

Uses: Perennial border, meadow, stream or pond side planting, shade garden and cut flower (depending on the species).

Evening primrose; see ***Oenothera***

Fairy candles; see ***Cimicifuga***

False lupine; see ***Thermopsis***

False Solomon's Seal; see ***Smilacina***

Filipendula rubra (fill-i-PEN-dew-lah RUE-bra) **queen-of-the-prairie,** Easy. ○

Origin: Eastern United States
Habitat: Moist meadows
Zones: 3 to 9
Height: 6 to 8 feet
Color: Pink
Characteristics: Filipendula rubra is a dramatic plant (reaching heights of 6 to 8 feet) with great divided leaves and big cotton candy–like inflorescences. The flowers, a salmon-pink color with a slight bubble gum fragrance, open during the month of July. This big, bold

Filipendula rubra

Gaillardia

plant never fails to receive compliments when seen in bloom. The variety 'Venusta' is the most common form available and has slightly deeper pink flowers than the species.

Cultural Information: In a rich, moist garden soil in full sun, queen-of-the-prairie will happily spread to form a mass about 5 feet wide. The great flower stems rarely need staking in sun, but in shadier spots the plant will need some support. When spacing young plants, give them plenty of room to grow because filipendula looks best when viewed in a mass. Set the plants 3 to 4 feet apart. Division is the easiest method to increase this plant and should be done in spring.

Uses: Perennial border, meadow, mass plantings.

Flowering raspberry; see *Rubus*

Foamflower; see *Tiarella*

Fringe-cup; see *Mitella*

Gaura lindheimeri

Fringed loosestrife; see *Lysimachia*

Fuchsia, California; see *Zauschneria*

Gaillardia (gay-LAR-dee-ah) **blanket flower,** Easy. ○ ◑ ☀ 🌡 ✿
Origin: Southern and western United States
Habitat: Dry meadows and prairies
Zones: 3 to 10
Height: 6 inches to 3 feet
Colors: Yellow, burgundy and combinations of both
Characteristics: The blanket flower begins flowering in late spring with vivid, hot-colored blooms, and keeps on going throughout the summer, making it one of the longest-blooming wildflowers. The most commonly available forms of gaillardia are hybrid crosses between the annual *Gaillardia pulchella* and the perennial *G. aristata* and are sold as *Gaillardia × grandiflora.* These crosses have the perennial nature of one parent along with the long bloom season of the other. There are many selections available such as 'Baby Cole' (a 7-inch-tall form that bears red flowers with yellow margins), 'Dazzler' (which grows to 2 feet and has golden flowers with crimson tips) and 'Goblin' (a 9- to 12-inch mounding plant with large red flowers with yellow edges).
Cultural Information: Gaillardias require full sun and will flower best in a rich, well-drained soil. Space the dwarf cultivars 8 inches apart, and the larger growing forms 12 to 15 inches apart. Deadhead the

plants regularly for the longest season of bloom. Taller selections may need staking. Gaillardias often last for only 2 to 3 years; it's almost as if they bloom themselves to death. Fortunately, most gaillardias are easily grown from seed and will flower in the first year. The cultivars 'Baby Cole' and 'Goblin', however, can only be propagated by division, which is best done in spring or fall.
Uses: Perennial garden, massing, groundcover.

Gaura lindheimeri (GAW-rah lind-HI-mer-eye) **gaura, wandflower,** Easy. ○ ◑ ☀ ✿
Origin: Louisiana and Texas
Habitat: Meadows
Zones: 6 to 10
Height: 3 to 4 feet
Color: White
Characteristics: The airy, butterflylike white flowers of gaura cluster along graceful, three-foot stems. While not a show stopper, gaura's long season of bloom (all summer long and into the fall), many dainty pink-budded white flowers, and drought tolerance should make this plant an essential in any dry perennial garden. *Gaura* makes a good foil for other showier blooms and can be used in the garden the way baby's breath is used in flower arrangements. A selection called 'Whirling Butterfly' is more floriferous and slightly shorter.
Cultural Information: Gaura is adapted to growing in dry sites by virtue of its deep taproot. Set young plants in a well-drained soil in full sun about 18 inches apart. Water consistently for the first season to en-

courage the growth of a good root system that will support the plant during periods of drought in future years. Additional plants may easily be grown from seed, which germinates in 2 to 3 weeks.

Uses: Perennial border, meadows, xeriscaping, massing, background plant.

Gayfeather; see *Liatris*

Geranium maculatum
(je-RAY-nee-um mak-you-LAY-tum) **wild geranium,** Easy. ○ ◑
Origin: Eastern North America
Habitat: Woodlands, moist meadows
Zones: 3 to 9
Height: 18 inches to 2 feet
Colors: Lavender-pink, white
Characteristics: Geranium maculatum frequents moist woods and meadows of the eastern United States. While not very showy in the wild, this pretty native is transformed when brought into cultivation. In a garden setting, the geranium forms a 2-foot mound that is completely covered with lavender-pink flowers in May. The palmately lobed leaves are ornamental all summer and turn a lovely shade of deep red in fall. This plant is little appreciated in American gardens, but Graham Stuart Thomas (the English "Dean of Perennials and Roses") describes it as a "first-class plant" and "in flower in May at which time there are few herbaceous plants to rival it." There is a white-flowered form called either variety *alba* or 'Hazel Gallagher'.
Cultural Information: To grow well, the wild geranium requires a moist, rich garden soil

in sun or light shade. If the soil dries out too much, this plant has the disconcerting habit of going dormant, but it will come back with vigor the next spring. Space the plants 2 feet apart. *Geranium maculatum* can be divided in spring or it can be grown from seed, which needs a period of moist, cold stratification in order to germinate. When well sited, the wild geranium will self-sow and seedlings can be moved to new homes or left to fill in the garden.
Uses: Perennial garden, woodland or shade garden, groundcover.

Geum triflorum (JEE-um try-FLOR-um) **prairie smoke,** Easy. ○ ◑ ◗ ❀
Origin: Western New York to Pacific coast
Habitat: Dry woods and prairies
Zones: 3 to 8
Height: 8 to 12 inches
Color: Rose-red
Characteristics: In late April, quaint red bell-like flowers emerge. One month later, the real beauty of the plant—the silvery pink seed plumes that give it its common name of prairie smoke—is revealed. Flowers are produced from late April to early June and seedheads are present from late May through July. The low, 4-inch hairy gray-green foliage of *Geum triflorum* remains an ornamental carpet for the remainder of the season.
Cultural Information: Geum triflorum prefers a rich, well-drained soil in full sun to light shade. Space plants approximately 12 inches apart. Seed requires a period of moist, cold

Geranium maculatum *'Hazel Gallagher' with* Aquilegia canadensis *var.* flava

Geranium maculatum *with* Endymion hispanica

Geum triflorum

stratification in order to germinate. Plants may also be divided in spring.

Uses: Rock garden, perennial border, groundcover.

Gillenia; see *Porteranthus*

Ginger, wild; see *Asarum*

Goat's beard; see *Aruncus*

Goldaster, hairy; see *Chrysopsis*

Goldenrod; see *Solidago*

Green and gold; see *Chrysogonum*

Hairy goldaster; see *Chrysopsis*

Hardy ageratum; see *Eupatorium*

Helenium (hel-LEAN-ee-um)
sneezeweed, Easy. ○ ▮ ✿
Origin: North America
Habitat: Meadows
Zones: 3 to 8
Height: 3 to 5 feet
Colors: Yellow, orange, mahogany
Characteristics: Great clusters of miniature sunflowers with toothed rays cover the sneezeweeds with color during the summer months. *Helenium autumnale,* the most commonly grown species, is native to moist meadows across the United States. Many cultivars of this plant exist in colors ranging from yellow to bronze to mahogany. It grows to a height of 4 to 5 feet. Despite its common name of sneezeweed, this plant does not cause hay fever. It just blooms at

Helenium hoopesii

about the same time as ragweed, which does cause allergy attacks. *H. hoopesii* is native to mountain meadows of the Pacific Northwest. From a fleshy basal rosette of leaves rise 2½-foot flower stalks in late June and July bearing clusters of orange flowers. It is a more refined plant than *H. autumnale,* but does not perform as well in the heat of the South.

Cultural Information: All heleniums prefer a moist, rich soil in full sun. *Helenium autumnale* may need staking, but is well worth the effort for its many weeks of showy flowers. Plants should be spaced about 3 feet apart for the *H. autumnale* and 12 inches apart for the *H. hoopesii.* Helenium seed requires a period of moist, cold stratification for germination, but be aware that seedlings of selected color forms may not have the same color as the parent plants. Division in spring or fall is another very easy method to increase stock.

Uses: Perennial border, meadow, cut flower.

Helianthus (heal-ee-AN-thus)
sunflower, Easy. ○ ✳ ▮ ✿
Origin: North America
Habitat: Meadows, prairies and woods
Zones: 3 to 9
Height: 3 to 10 feet
Colors: Yellow, gold, orange, cream
Characteristics: I can think of no other flower that brings a smile to everyone's lips the way sunflowers do. Their open, sunny countenance brings warmth and pleasure to all who behold them. There are many members of the sunflower genus that are ornamental, long-blooming garden flowers. Perhaps the best known is *Helianthus annus* (the sunflower from which edible sunflower seeds come). Hybridizers have worked away at this species to produce everything from great 10-foot giants with 1-foot-wide flowers to dwarfer specimens with multicolored blooms. A few of the showiest perennial species include hybrids of the eastern *H. decapetalus* and the annual sunflower called *H. × multiflorus.* They

Helianthus mollis *with*
Panicum virgatum
'Haense Hermes'

flower in summer with golden-yellow blossoms. 'Multiflorus' is an old-fashioned double-flowered form that reaches 6 to 8 feet. Newer selections such as the semidouble 'Meteor' and the double 'Loddon Gold' grow to only 4 to 5 feet. *H. salicifolius*, from the central United States, is grown more for its gracefully whorled and drooping lilylike foliage than for its flowers. It reaches a height of 6 to 8 feet, prefers moist soils and produces yellow flowers in late summer and early fall. The foliage of this willowleaf sunflower makes a magnificent contrast to other tall-growing perennials and ornamental grasses. *H. mollis*, of the western United States, is an extremely drought-tolerant sunflower that has hairy grayish foliage, grows 3 to 3½ feet tall and bears many buttercup-yellow blossoms in midsummer. *H. angustifolius* is a 5-foot southeastern native with narrow, dark green glossy leaves with numerous yellow flowers in late fall. This plant is hardy only to Zone 6 but is useful for its late season of bloom.

Cultural Information: Sunflowers are easy to grow in rich garden soil in full sun. A few species such as *Helianthus angustifolius* and *H. salicifolius* do best in moist soil, while *H. mollis* is tolerant of extremely dry conditions. Give the plants room to grow by spacing them about 3 feet apart. Birds love the seeds so don't deadhead the flowers too quickly. New plants are easily grown from seed or by division.

Uses: Perennial border, meadow, cut flower.

Heliopsis helianthoides

(heal-ee-OP-sis   heal-ee-an-THOI-deez) **ox-eye sunflower,** Easy.

○ ◗ ❀

Origin: Eastern United States

Habitat: Thickets and stream banks

Zones: 4 to 9

Height: 4 to 5 feet

Color: Golden yellow

Characteristics: Heliopsis is an extremely long-flowering, summer-blooming plant. If deadheaded, it can produce flowers from July through the end of September. In a town near my home, someone has lined a white picket fence with heliopsis. It is a joy to see the sunny yellow blossoms poking up above and through the fence all summer long. Many cultivars exist including 'Incomparabilis', which grows to 3 feet and bears orange-yellow semidouble flowers, 'Golden Greenheart', which has double yellow blossoms with green centers and 'Karat', which has large, single, deep golden blossoms. I prefer the single forms because they seem lighter and more graceful and they bloom for a longer time than the doubles.

Cultural Information: Heliopsis performs best in a rich, moist to average garden soil in full sun. In partial shade or in warmer climates, plants may need staking. Set plants about 2½ feet apart in the garden. Although the species may be grown from seed, which requires a period of moist, cold stratification in order to germinate, named cultivars must be increased by division in spring or fall.

Uses: Perennial garden, meadows, cut flower.

Heliopsis helianthoides

Heuchera micrantha

Heuchera (HUE-kuh-rah) **alumroot, coral bells,** Easy.

○ ◑ ❀

Origin: North America

Habitat: Rocky outcrops

Zones: 3 to 9

Height: 18 to 30 inches

Colors: White, pink, rose-red, salmon

Characteristics: Scalloped evergreen foliage and airy spikes bearing many tiny flowers make this a useful and graceful addition to rock gardens and perennial borders. The most commonly grown coral bells are known collectively as *H. × brizoides.* They are the result of hybridizing *H. micrantha* from the Pacific states, *H. sanguinea* from Arizona and New Mexico and *H. americana* from the East. The result is many beautiful hybrids bearing white, pink and rose-colored blossoms in May and June. 'White Cloud' is a vigorous white form, 'Chatterbox' has large pink flowers and 'Mt. St. Helens' bears brilliant red blossoms. Several of the species of heuchera are equally garden worthy yet much less commonly grown. *H. americana* has large green leaves, often attractively mottled with gray. This plant prefers a site in partial shade. There it produces creamy white flowers that are not all that showy but provide a quiet display of bloom all summer long. *H. micrantha* is a similar plant bearing greenish-white flowers. Recently, a deep purple-leafed heuchera known as 'Palace Purple', has taken the perennial world by storm. Although there is much controversy over its parentage, it bears white flowers all summer long as do either *H. micrantha* or *H. americana.* This plant should be sited in a sunny position in order for the leaves to stay dark purple.

Cultural Information: Heuchera × brizoides should be grown in a rich, well-drained soil in full sun to light shade. *H. americana* and *H. micrantha* do best in part shade in a similar rich, well-drained soil. Space the plants 18 to 24 inches apart. Named cultivars can be propagated by division in spring, while the species are easily

Hibiscus palustris

grown from seed, which requires a period of moist, cold stratification in order to germinate.

Uses: Perennial border, rock garden, shade or woodland garden, cut flower.

Hibiscus (hih-BIS-kus) rose mallow, Easy. ○

Origin: Eastern and central United States

Habitat: Marshes

Zones: 4 to 9

Height: 2 to 6 feet

Colors: White, pink, rose-red

Characteristics: While most tropical hibiscus are shrubs, the native rose mallows are deciduous, dying to the ground only to resprout once the soil is warm in the spring. They quickly grow into 5-foot rounded bushes covered with large flowers in late summer. The taxonomy is a bit confused, but plants with white flowers and dark red centers are often called *Hibiscus moscheutos,* while pink and rose-colored forms are known as *H. palustris.* Recently, new hybrids

have been developed that have larger, flattened flowers in brighter colors and sometimes dwarfer habits of growth. 'Lord Baltimore' has bright red flowers and the 'Disco Belle' series bears huge flowers in pink, red or white on 2-foot plants. I am fond of the smaller, cup-shaped flowers of the species that are less tropical looking than the flatter hybrid blossoms. Certainly the species are more appropriate for natural-looking gardens.

Cultural Information: Hibiscus grow best in rich, moist to average garden soil in full sun. Space these vigorous beauties 4 to 5 feet apart. Plants may be grown quite easily from seed that germinates fastest if soaked in warm water for 24 hours before sowing. Theoretically, if there were a color form that you particularly liked, you could divide the plant; but be aware that the hibiscus are quite woody at their base and would require a saw and a lot of elbow grease to pry into pieces.

Uses: Perennial garden, shrub border, meadows, damp gardens and pond side plantings.

Hoary mountain mint; see *Pycnanthemum*

Indian physic; see *Porteranthus*

Inside-out flower; see *Vancouveria*

Iris ((EYE-ris) **iris,** Easy. ○ ◑ ⬤
Origin: Throughout the United States
Habitat: Meadows, woods
Zones: 4 to 10
Height: 4 inches to 4 feet
Colors: Blue, white, yellow, coppery red, violet
Characteristics: North America has many lovely irises in rich and varied shades of color, inhabiting many different locales from swamps to meadows to woodlands. No matter where you live there is a native iris that will thrive in your garden. Many of these species have been ignored as people have concentrated on the more familiar German bearded irises. Below are a few types of native irises deserving a place in American gardens.

Iris versicolor (eastern blue flag) is native to wet meadows throughout the Northeast. It bears many 2-foot, violet-blue blossoms in late May or June. Deep lavender and white forms are available from specialty nurseries. It grows best in a moist, sunny, slightly acid site in the garden.

Iris virginica (southern blue flag) looks like a more robust version of *I. versicolor.* It grows in similar moist sunny spots in the Southeast and up the Mississippi River valley.

Iris setosa canadensis is a pretty little 10-inch plant with blue-purple flowers appearing in late May and early June. This dwarf beauty is native to moist, somewhat acid soils along the coast of Maine. It is hardy to Zone 3.

Iris missouriensis (western blue flag) looks fairly similar to the eastern blue flags, with blue flowers that have a touch of yellow on their falls. It is found in moist meadows in full sun although it can tolerate drier conditions later in the season.

Iris cristata (dwarf crested iris) is native to woodlands of the Southeast. This tiny 4- to 6-inch-tall plant prefers a moist but well-drained soil in partial shade. It is a rapid spreader, forming a dense groundcover of green iris fans above which rise blue flowers with distinctive yellow crests in May. This is a terrific groundcover for shady gardens and is hardy in Zones 3 to 9. A white form is commonly available, and lighter and darker blue forms have also been introduced recently.

Iris cristata

The dry, slightly shady hillsides of California and Oregon are home to some dozen species of California iris ranging in color from blues to yellows to cream, often with contrasting colored veins on the falls. Most reach about 2 feet and are easily grown in a slightly shaded spot that is rich in organic matter. Much hybridizing is being done with these species and many new color forms and plants with more vigorous habits of growth have been introduced. These new and exciting plants are referred to as Pacific Coast hybrids and are hardy in Zones 7 to 9.
Cultural Information: Irises are best divided in late summer. They may also be grown from seed, which needs a period of moist, cold stratification in order to germinate.
Uses: Pond side plantings, damp gardens, perennial borders, shade gardens, cut flower.

Louisiana Irises

This group of irises has a most fascinating bit of American history attached to it. The story lies with a group of 5 species of iris native to a relatively small area of south central Louisiana and the nearby Gulf Coast. One of these species, Iris fulva, *was a unique coppery red, a color unknown in any other iris. The 5 species hybridized freely among themselves for centuries, producing the most varied array of colors of any irises in the world ranging from white and yellow to pinks, rose, copper, red, intense blues and deep lavenders. Credit for the discovery of these irises is usually given to John K. Small, a curator at the New York Botanical Garden, who first observed the natural stands from a train window in the 1920s. He dubbed Louisiana the "Iris Center of the Universe" and spurred a number of local wildflower enthusiasts into combing the swamps looking for the most interesting of the hybrids. This period of wild collecting lasted into the 1950s. While collection of* plants in the wild is frowned upon today, most of these beautiful hybrids would have been lost to development were it not for the efforts of a handful of people.

As their popularity expands, Louisiana irises are now grown in much of the United States as well as in other parts of the world. They are particularly popular in warm regions where bearded irises do not do well. Interestingly, they have proved hardy much farther north than their native habitat—even into Zone 4—with protection. I have happily grown a selection of these hybrids for several years in New York in Zone 5. In warmer climates they bloom as early as April—they flower for me in late June and early July.

Louisiana irises like a humus-rich, slightly acid soil and full sun. They can grow in very moist conditions and even in shallow water. They can also be grown in a moist, rich perennial border. Most forms are vigorous growers and should be given plenty of space, so plant them about 30 to 36 inches apart.

Louisiana Iris *'Peggy Mae'*

Ironweed; see **Vernonia**

Jack-in-the-pulpit; see **Arisaema**

Jacob's ladder; see **Polemonium**

Joe Pye weed; see **Eupatorium**

Leadplant; see **Amorpha**

Liatris (lee-AH-tris) **blazing star, gayfeather,** Easy. ○ 🔔
Origin: Eastern two-thirds of the United States
Habitat: Wet or dry meadows and prairies
Zones: 3 to 9
Height: 2 to 5 feet
Colors: Rose-lavender to purple
Characteristics: No other plant in my nursery attracts more birds with its seed than the lovely liatris. When I harvest the seeds, goldfinches will remain within 2 feet of my hands as they greedily gulp down the thistlelike seed. Recently, Dutch bulb companies have begun selling the tuberous roots of li- atris along with daffodils and tulips. While the glossy photos in fall bulb catalogs popularize the showy lavender spikes of the blazing star, few people are aware that the *Liatris* genus is native to North America. Although there are more than 40 species in the genus, only one species, *Liatris spicata,* is commonly available. It is characterized by a very dense cluster

Liatris spicata *'Kobold'*

of showy purple blossoms that reach a height of 4 feet. There is a dwarf selection called 'Kobold', which is only 24 to 30 inches tall, and a white form known as 'Floristan White'. Pretty as *L. spicata* is, I much prefer the looser and longer stalked flowers of another species, *L. ligustylis* (meadow blazing star). Sometimes the flower spikes even branch, making for a very graceful flower form. In my opinion, the showiest of all the liatris is the little-known New England blazing star (*L. novae-angliae*), which has very large spidery flowers on long stalks. I hope some of these less common beauties find their way to the marketplace in the near future.

Cultural Information: Liatris are quite adaptable plants but perform their best in full sun in rich, slightly moist garden soil. Space plants about 18 inches apart. The taller forms usually need staking, but sometimes I allow them to flop down and then snake upward to the light because they do it so gracefully. Plants may be increased by division in spring or fall and they can easily be grown from seed, which requires a period of moist stratification in order to germinate.

Uses: Perennial border, wildflower meadow or prairie, cut flowers, attracts birds.

Lilium (LIL-ee-um) **lily,** Moderate. ○ ◐ ▮

Origin: Throughout the United States

Habitat: Moist meadows and wood edges

Zones: 4 to 8

Height: 4 to 6 feet

Colors: Yellow, orange, red

Characteristics: For centuries lilies, which are found throughout the northern hemisphere, have been admired by gardeners and artists for their elegance and fragrance. North America can boast of quite a few lilies growing wild from coast to coast, but unfortunately only two native species are generally available from nurseries that propagate their stock rather than collect the plants from the wild. These two commercially available species are native to the eastern United States. *Lilium canadense* (Canada lily) comes in a variety of colors ranging from pure yellow to orange to a deep red. *L. superbum* (turk's cap lily) is very similar but has strongly reflexed petals similar in shape to those of the tiger lily. It is usually found in an orange color. Both lilies bloom in July and reach 4 to 6 feet.

Cultural Information: The Canada lily and the Turk's cap lily both inhabit moist meadows and wood edges in the wild. Plant the bulbs in fall in a moist, humus-rich site in full sun to partial shade. These lilies look best when planted in groups or colonies. I have found the Turk's cap lily easier to establish than the Canada lily. Plants may be propagated by offsets from the mother bulb or from seed. In each case it will be a few to many years until the plants are mature enough to flower.

Uses: Meadows, perennial gardens, cut flower.

Lily; see *Lilium*

Lilium superbum

Lobelia cardinalis

Lobelia (low-BEE-lee-ah) **lobelia, cardinal flower,** Easy. ○ ◐ ❀

Origin: North America

Habitat: Moist woods and meadows

Zones: 2 to 9

Height: 2 to 4 feet

Colors: White, pink, rose, red, blue, purple

Characteristics: The brilliant red spikes of the cardinal

flower (*Lobelia cardinalis*) brighten moist woods in late summer throughout the United States. The cardinal flower has long been loved by wildflower enthusiasts as much for its showy blossoms as for its ability to attract hummingbirds to the garden. There are a number of other native lobelia species, but the only other one that really merits the attention of the gardener is *Lobelia siphilitica* (great blue lobelia), which looks like a sky blue version of the cardinal flower. This plant will self-sow profusely about the garden. For this reason and because it tends to be short-lived, some people frown upon this plant. However, I am a great fan of *L. siphilitica*; even though an individual plant may not remain for long, there will always be new plants nearby. I like to have a few flowers that will intermingle among my "placed" plants because they give the planned garden a more natural feel. Besides, the unwanted seedlings are easily removed in spring, and a touch of blue here or there in the fall makes for wonderful contrasts. In the wild the two species, red and blue, will occasionally cross-pollinate, producing offspring of various hues. Several people in Canada and North Carolina have begun doing controlled crosses between the two species and they have also been selecting for superior color forms of the species themselves. The results have been spectacular with flowers ranging from rose-pink to vivid ruby to deep velvety purples. *Cultural Information:* Lobelia cardinalis and *L. siphilitica* like

Lupinus *species*

a humus-rich, slightly to very moist garden soil in sun or light shade. In hotter climates they will do better in partial shade. Space the plants 18 inches apart. New plants are easily grown from seed, which requires a moist, cold period of stratification in order to germinate. Superior color forms may be increased by division in the spring.
Uses: Perennial border, shade garden, pond side or damp garden.

Loosestrife, fringed; see *Lysimachia*

Lupine; see *Lupinus*

Lupine, false; see *Thermopsis*

Lupinus (lew-PIE-nus) **lupine,** Difficult. ○ ◐ ◕ ❀
Origin: Throughout the United States
Habitat: Sunny meadows
Zones: 4 to 9

Height: 6 inches to 4 feet
Colors: Blue, yellow, white, pink
Characteristics: There are many beautiful species of lupines native to the United States, particularly in the western states. Few are commonly grown in gardens because lupines resent having their roots disturbed. The key is to plant young seedlings grown in individual pots, which will reduce the shock of transplanting. *Lupinus perennis* is the beloved blue lupine of the East, while *L. texensis* is the famous Texas bluebonnet that carpets fields in spring. *L. arborescens*, a lovely, yellow-flowering tree lupine native to California, is happiest in well-drained soil in gardens along the West Coast. An Englishman by the name of Russell crossed a number of western American lupine species to produce a popular group of plants known as the Russell hybrids. These lupines come in a great range of colors from white and yellow to pinks, blues and purples, and sometimes in two tones.

The Russell lupines are quite showy in the garden but are often short lived, especially in hotter, wetter climates.

Cultural Information: Most lupines like full sun and a well-drained, acid soil. To establish plants in your garden or meadow it is best to either sow seeds directly where they are to grow in the ground or to sow the seeds in individual pots in order to keep transplanting shock to a minimum. In either case, soak the seeds for 24 hours in warm water before sowing. Spacing will vary according to the species, with dwarf growers needing to be closer and 4-foot specimens farther apart; however, a general rule of thumb is to space potted plants about 2 feet apart.

Uses: Perennial garden, meadow.

Lysimachia ciliata (li-si-MOCK-ee-ah sil-lee-ATE-ah) **fringed loosestrife,** Easy. ○ ◑

Origin: Eastern United States
Habitat: Moist woods and fields
Zones: 4 to 9
Height: 3 to 4 feet
Color: Yellow
Characteristics: This plant is common in moist woods in the East. While it is pretty in the garden, it can be very invasive. It is best used in moist sunny or shady sites that need a naturalistic groundcover, (along the edge of a pond, for example). A deep purple–leafed form has only recently been introduced as variety *purpurea. Lysimachia ciliata* var. *purpurea* and *Heuchera* 'Palace Purple' are the only two native plants that have this lovely purple foliage. In July, the pendulous yellow bell-shaped flowers dangling from the leaf axils only serve to enhance the dramatic purple foliage.

Cultural Information: Lysimachia ciliata can be grown in full sun but it requires constant moisture or it will wilt. It is otherwise undemanding of soil type, but will grow fastest when the site is rich with organic matter. Lysimachia is also tolerant of a fair amount of shade, providing it has some moisture. The purple-leafed form needs full sun to obtain its best color. Variety *purpurea* is not as invasive as the species, but it still is a robust grower and will quickly form a good-sized colony. In order to reduce self-sowing, cut back the flowers to the basal rosettes before they set seed. Space plants 3 feet apart. The easiest way to propagate this plant is by division in spring or fall.

Uses: Perennial garden, damp garden, naturalizing in moist areas.

Mayapple; see ***Podophyllum***

Meadow-rue, tall; see ***Thalictrum***

Mealy-cup sage; see ***Salvia***

Merrybells; see ***Uvularia***

Mertensia virginica (mer-TEN-see-ah vir-JIN-i-kah) **Virginia bluebells,** Easy. ◑

Origin: Eastern United States
Habitat: Moist woods
Zones: 3 to 9
Height: 18 inches to 2 feet
Colors: Pink changing to blue
Characteristics: Virginia blue-

Lysimachia ciliata

Mertensia virginica

bells are one of the great joys of the spring garden. The plant's blue-green leaves emerge from the ground in May and are quickly followed by pink buds that gradually open to nodding, lavender, bluebell-like flowers. In the wild this plant is found in moist, rich woods and it prefers a similar site in the garden. Under such conditions, the mertensia will self-sow and the individual plants will soon spread to form a very pretty colony. *Mertensia* turns yellow and goes dormant soon after setting seed, sometime in midsummer, so it is best to place it in the background of a planting where an empty space will be less noticeable. It is a vigorous grower and has no problem coming up each year through a permanent groundcover such as *Vinca minor* (periwinkle) or *Phlox stolonifera*.

Cultural Information: Plant *Mertensia virginica* 2 feet apart in a rich, somewhat moist soil in partial shade. Personal experience has taught me that mertensia can be divided after flowering, but do it soon because once the plants are dormant, you won't be able to find them until the next spring.

Uses: Woodland and shade gardens, naturalizing.

Milkweed; see *Asclepias*

Mimulus guttatus (MIM-you-lus gut-TOT-us) **monkey flower,** Easy. ○ ◑ ✿

Origin: Western United States
Habitat: Wet areas
Zones: 5 to 8
Height: 4 inches to 3 feet
Color: Yellow
Characteristics: The cheerful yellow blossoms of the monkey flower brighten many moist areas from early spring through

Mimulus guttatus

fall. *Mimulus guttatus* has fleshy stems that sometimes can rise to a height of 3 feet and at other times may lay along the ground depending upon the moisture, richness of the soil and amount of sunlight. Plants self-sow profusely and make a fine groundcover for moist areas. They combine well with Japanese primroses.

Cultural Information: Plant the monkey flower in a constantly moist site in full sun or light shade. The easiest way to propagate this plant is by division in spring or fall or by digging and moving some of the many new seedlings that appear each year. Space plants 12 to 18 inches apart.

Uses: Pond or stream-side plantings, damp garden, groundcover.

Mint, hoary mountain; see *Pycnanthemum*

Mitella* and *Tellima (my-TELL-ah) and (TELL-i-mah) **miterwort** and **fringe-cup,** Easy. ◑ ●

Origin: North America
Habitat: Damp woods
Zones: 4 to 8
Height: 12 to 18 inches
Color: White
Characteristics: *Mitella diphylla* is found in the eastern half of the United States, while *Tellima grandiflora* is native to the Pacific Northwest. They are almost identical, but have been separated into two genera by taxonomists (*Tellima* actually is an anagram of *Mitella*). As far as gardeners are concerned, the two plants can be grouped together. Both have heart-shaped evergreen leaves and bear 10- to 12-inch spikes of greenish-

Tellima grandiflora

white flowers. The individual flowers are not very large, but they are extremely beautiful when observed closely because they resemble tiny snowflakes. The overall effect of the plant is like that of a heuchera. Tellima is a slightly more robust grower, but both make good garden plants and groundcovers for a woodland or shade garden. In winter the foliage takes on a reddish tone, which is more pronounced when the plant receives some sunlight.

Cultural Information: Grow mitella and tellima in partial shade in moist soil that is rich in organic matter. Space the plants 18 inches apart. Both species are more effective in the garden when massed. They are easily grown from seed, which requires a period of moist, cold stratification in order to germinate or they can be divided in the spring.

Uses: Woodland or shade garden, groundcover.

Miterwort; see *Mitella*

Monarda (moe-NAR-dah) **bee-balm, oswego tea, wild bergamot,** Easy. ○ ◑ 🌡 ❀
Origin: Eastern United States
Habitat: Meadows and fields
Zones: 4 to 9
Height: 2 to 4 feet
Colors: Red, lavender, pink, white, purple
Characteristics: Monarda didyma, (beebalm) is grown by many gardeners for its brilliant red tubular flowers that bloom in July and serve to attract hummingbirds. A close relative of this plant is *M. fistulosa* (wild bergamot), a lavender-flowered version that is commonly found in the wild in drier locations than its cousin. Monardas are in the mint family and fragrant leaves of the red monarda were supposedly used as a tea substitute during the American Revolution, hence its other common name of Oswego tea. *M. didyma* does have one important flaw as a garden plant: It is incredibly invasive. Wild bergamot is not so vigorous, but its pale lavender flowers can be uninspiring. There are, however, a vast array of selections and hybrids between the two that are better behaved in the garden and that come in a wide range of colors. For example, 'Adam' is a dwarfer cherry red, 'Croftway Pink' is a clear pink and 'Blue Stocking' is a deep lavender-blue.

In my opinion, the most beautiful of the monardas is a relatively unknown species, *M. punctata* (Horsemint), which inhabits sandy coastal areas from Long Island south to Florida. This plant blooms from August through October with pretty little yellow spotted flowers. Its loveliness lies not in the flowers but in the silver to dusty rose bracts that circle the base of the blossoms. The plant is in bloom so long because as one flower finishes, another emerges on top; meanwhile, the showy bracts underneath each flower remain ornamental for several months.
Cultural Information: Monarda didyma, M. fistulosa and cultivars perform best in full sun in a rich, organic soil. In areas with high humidity, mildew can be a problem, so it is a good idea to select for cultivars that are less prone to mildew and also to site the plant where there is good air circulation. Space the plants 3 feet apart. These plants are easily divided in spring or fall. *M. punctata* prefers a well-drained soil in full sun. It is a dwarfer plant, reaching only about 2 feet in height and the same in width, so space it 18 inches apart. When happy, *M. punctata* will self-sow. The young seedlings can be moved from place to place around the garden. Monarda seed does not need any pretreatment in order to germinate.
Uses: Perennial border, meadow, cut flower, dried flower.

Monkey flower; see *Mimulus*

Mountain mint, hoary; see *Pycnanthemume*

Nodding pink onion; see *Allium*

Monarda punctata

Oenothera fruticosa

Oenothera (ee-no-THAIR-ah) **sundrops, evening primrose,** Easy. ○ 💧 ✳ 🌡 ❀
Origin: North America
Habitat: Fields and prairies
Zones: 4 to 9
Height: 8 inches to 2 feet
Colors: White, pink, yellow
Characteristics: The sunny yellow blossoms of the sundrops brighten many gardens in late spring. For decades, gardeners have shared divisions of this plant with friends and family. Its ease of culture and showy flowers make it popular everywhere. The taxonomy of this plant is quite confused and one

can buy it under the name of *Oenothera perennis, O. fruticosa* or *O. tetragona.* Another popular oenothera is *O. speciosa,* the showy evening primrose. This plant bears many pale pink flowers in spring. It is particularly dramatic in the fields in Texas, where it forms great masses and combines beautifully with the wild blue lupines that bloom at the same time. In the garden *O. speciosa* is easy to grow, but it should be planted with care because it is an extremely vigorous spreader and is best used where a fast-growing groundcover is needed. *Cultural Information:* The yellow sundrops prefers a moist to average garden soil in full sun but it will also tolerate light shade. It is a fast grower (although not as fast as *O. speciosa*), and can be spaced 2 feet or more apart. *O. speciosa* is tolerant of drier conditions and very sunny warm spots. The roots creep rapidly to form a great colony. Both species should be cut back after flowering since the old flower stalks soon look untidy. Division in spring or fall is the easiest way to increase your plants.
Uses: Sunny perennial garden, meadow, groundcover, cut flower.

Onion, nodding pink; see *Allium*

Opuntia (oh-PUN-tee-ah) **prickly pear,** Easy. ○ ◗ ✳
Origin: Most of the United States
Habitat: Dry sandy or rocky soils
Zones: 5 to 10
Height: 6 to 8 inches

Opuntia humifusa

Colors: Yellow, orange
Characteristics: Almost all members of the cactus family are native to the Americas. Of these, most species are native to the southwestern United States, Mexico or South America. Only one genus, *Opuntia,* is found growing throughout most of the United States. The distinctive pear-shaped pads, one on top of another, give it its common name of prickly pear. The opuntias are also the most adaptable of the native cacti; they grow easily in a variety of climates, whether hot or cold. All they require is sandy, well-drained soil and plenty of sunshine. The most commonly available species is *Opuntia humifusa,* which is native from Massachusetts to Florida to Montana. In the wild, the flower is a double pale yellow blossom often with an orange center. There are orange-flowered forms available from some nurseries as well. The individual pear-shaped pads are about 4 inches long. The pads tend to lie along the ground, so the plant remains at a height of about 4 to 6 inches. Flowers occur in June and July.
Cultural Information: Opuntias require a sandy, well-drained soil in full sun for survival. Plants purchased in pots should be spaced about 1 foot apart and watered consistently for the first season to encourage the growth of deeper and more wide-spreading roots. Once established, the prickly pear will need little or no water. Keep an eye out for weeds and remove them instantly before they have a chance to get established. Once weeds become intertwined with the spiny pads of the cactus, they are almost impossible to eradicate. You can also establish a colony of prickly pear by breaking off several pads in spring, allowing the wound to form a callous by setting the pads in a dry, airy spot for a day or so and then inserting the pads, broken part down, into the sandy garden soil. Keep well watered for the first season as the pads develop their roots.
Uses: Perennial gardens, extremely dry sandy situations such as a beach house, xeriscapes.

Oswego tea; see *Monarda*

Pachysandra procumbens (pack-i-SAN-drah pro-KUM-benz) **Allegheny spurge,** Moderate. ◐ ●

Origin: Southeastern United States
Habitat: Rich woods
Zones: 5 to 9
Height: 1 foot
Color: White
Characteristics: Pachysandra procumbens is the native pachysandra. The more commonly grown groundcover comes from Japan. Unlike the Japanese pachysandra, the native species is not a vigorous colonizer. Instead, it slowly spreads to form a small but dense colony. Allegheny spurge is a beautiful plant with 4-season interest. In spring, 4- to 6-inch spikes of white flowers arise from among last year's leaves. They are soon followed by the fresh green shoots of the new leaves, which ultimately reach a height of 12 inches and unfurl to be a cool gray-green color all summer. In autumn the leaves sink to the ground and turn a mottled purple-green, remaining ornamental all winter in warmer climates and half the winter in Zone 5.
Cultural Information: Give the Allegheny spurge a humus-rich, moist soil in semishade. For best effect, plant this pachysandra in small groups or drifts. Space plants 8 inches apart. Division in spring is the way to propagate.
Uses: Shade or woodland garden, groundcover for small areas.

Penstemon (PEN-ste-mon) **beard-tongue,** Easy, Moderate or Difficult (depending on the species). ○ ✿

Origin: North America
Habitat: Sunny meadows, prairies and rock outcrops
Zones: 3 to 9
Height: 6 inches to 4 feet
Colors: White, pinks, rose, reds, blues and lavenders
Characteristics: The penstemons comprise a huge genus of 250 species, all but one of which are native to North America, and most of which are found growing in the western United States. Penstemons are members of the snapdragon and foxglove family and bear the characteristic showy tubular flowers in an extraordinarily wide range of colors, from pinks and reds to blues and lavenders as well as white. Penstemons are native to eastern moist meadows, sandy coastal sites, prairies and dry rocky outcrops in the West. Some species, although beautiful, are very fussy about soil and drainage, but the ones discussed here are easy to grow in most perennial gardens.

The most commonly grown beard-tongues are hybrids and selections of *Penstemon barbatus,* which has very showy red blossoms. Native to the southwestern United States (where it is common in the mountains) it is quite hardy (to Zone 3) and is also very heat tolerant. 'Rose Elf' is a rose-colored cultivar, 'Prairie Fire' bears brilliant red tubular flowers and 'Prairie Dawn' has softer pale pink blossoms. *P. digitalis* (foxglove beard-tongue) is a showy white-flowered plant that inhabits moist meadows in the East. This plant has become very popular lately due to a new introduction by the University of Nebraska, appropriately named 'Husker's Red'. This form has burgundy-colored leaves, which make a wonderful contrast with other plants in the perennial border. Another easterner, *P. hirsutus* (hairy beardtongue), bears many delicate lavender blossoms in spring and reaches a height of 2 feet. There is a dwarf variety of this plant sold as 'Pygmeus', which flowers

Penstemon *'Prairie Fire'*
with Eupatorium capillifolium

Pachysandra procumbens

when the plant reaches 6 inches. *P. smallii*, from the Southeast, bears many rose-pink blossoms starting in May; if deadheaded, it will continue to bloom through the fall. Plants tend to be short-lived but will self-sow to a limited extent. *P. grandiflorus* is a showy species from the prairie states that bears enormous sky-blue flowers in June. This plant also has very ornamental gray-green leaves. It prefers a well-drained, sunny site.

Cultural Information: Most penstemons from the East grow easily in average garden soil in full sun. Those from the western United States generally demand good drainage, especially in winter. Many of the beautiful western plants are quite fussy and need specially prepared beds of gravel and sand that mimic the dry hillsides where they grow in the wild. Depending upon the ultimate size of the plants, penstemons should be spaced 12 to 18 inches apart. The species can be grown from seed, which requires a period of moist, cold stratification for germination. Selected color forms must be propagated by division in spring.

Uses: Perennial border, meadow, rock garden.

Phlox (FLOCKS) **phlox,** Easy.
○ ◑ ❶ ❀

Origin: North America
Habitat: Woodlands, meadows, rock outcrops
Zones: 3 to 9
Height: 4 inches to 4 feet
Colors: White, pink, blue, lavender
Characteristics: There are 60

Phlox divaricata

species of phlox, all but one of which are native to North America. The most commonly grown is *Phlox paniculata*, the so-called garden phlox, which bears great rounded fragrant blossoms in midsummer. While certainly worthy of a spot in every garden, this beauty does have one flaw. Its foliage is highly prone to mildew, especially in humid climates. There are many other lovely species of phlox that are disease-resistant and lower growing and deserve more popular attention.

First to bloom are the moss pinks, *P. subulata*. This low-growing, 6-inch plant has prickly green foliage that is covered with pink, white or blue blossoms in early spring. These plants are easily grown in sunny, well-drained soil. They spread quickly to form a dense groundcovering mat.

Next to flower are the woodland phloxes: *P. stolonifera*, which creeps along the ground, and *P. divaricata*, which reaches a height of 12 inches.

Both bear similar rounded inflorescences of blue, white or pink flowers and prefer a rich, moist soil in partial shade. The woodland phloxes are easy to grow and provide a long, spectacular mass of color in the spring shade garden. All of the woodland phloxes have a light fragrance that is more pronounced when they are massed, but I have found the *P. divaricata* cultivar 'Fuller's White' to be one of the most fragrant of all the plants I grow.

Blooming in late spring is a group of less well known phloxes that are usually lumped into the *Phlox glaberrima* group (although they may be hybrids of a few related species). Plants in this group can be purchased under the names *P. glaberrima*, *P.* 'Morris Berd' and *P.* 'Spring Delight', among others. They form 1-foot mounds of bright pink to light pink blossoms and do best in sun to partial shade.

P. maculata flowers in late spring to early summer. It is a taller growing plant, usually reaching a height of 3 feet. The flowers of this phlox are similar to those of the garden phlox but are more columnar in shape. Its glossy green foliage does not have a mildew problem. 'Miss Lingard' is a pure white form that often blooms again in late summer.

In July and August, the garden phloxes (*P. paniculata*) blossom with great rounded heads of flowers at a height of 3 to 4 feet. Much work has been done on this native American species in England and we can now grow such showy forms as 'Bright Eyes', which has pale pink flowers with a crimson eye, 'Starfire' with brilliant cherry red blossoms and 'Mt. Fuji' with huge white clusters of flowers.

Cultural Information: The moss pinks (*Phlox subulata*) require a well-drained soil in full sun. The woodland phloxes like a partially shaded site that is moist and rich in organic matter. The *P. glaberrima* cultivars, *P. maculata* cultivars and *P. paniculata* grow best in a rich garden soil in full sun to light shade. Try to site *P. paniculata* in a spot with good air circulation so the foliage will be less prone to mildew. The lower growing phloxes should be planted 12 to 18 inches apart while the tall growing phloxes should be spaced 3 to 4 feet apart. Phloxes can be propagated by division in spring or from stem cuttings taken in late spring.

Uses: Shade or woodland garden, rock garden, perennial border, cut flower.

Pink; see *Silene*

Podophyllum peltatum
(po-do-PHYL-um   pel-TAY-tum)
mayapple, Easy. ◐ ●
Origin: Eastern United States
Habitat: Rich woods
Zones: 3 to 8
Height: 18 to 24 inches
Color: White
Characteristics: *Podophyllum peltatum* is remarkable for its shiny green leaves, which emerge from the ground like a closed umbrella and gradually open to form a 2-foot-tall parasol. Underneath each of these umbrellalike leaves is a single nodding white flower best seen from a prone position on the ground. Later on, the podophyllum produces a greenish round fruit that gives it its common name of mayapple. Be forewarned that this plant is a vigorous colonizer that spreads by underground stems. It also goes dormant in midsummer. Although these two characteristics could be considered faults, the mayapple is very useful when sited correctly. In the woodland garden it makes a great transition between intensively cultivated plantings and more natural woods. In such a spot it can be allowed to spread freely, and it will form a beautiful backdrop for early spring flowers.

Cultural Information: Mayapples should be grown in a rich soil that is moist in spring. It grows fastest in partial shade but is tolerant of fairly dense shade as well. Space plants about 3 feet apart. The easiest way to propagate this plant is by division, which should be done before the plants go dormant in midsummer.

Podophyllum peltatum

Polemonium reptans *with* Dicentra eximia

Uses: Woodland gardens, groundcover.

Polemonium (pol-e-MOAN-ee-um) **creeping valerian, Jacob's ladder,** Easy. ○ ◐
Origin: North America
Habitat: Woodlands
Zones: 2 to 8
Height: 1 to 2 feet
Colors: Blue, white
Characteristics: Polemoniums have ornamental, ladderlike leaves above which rise nodding bluebell-like flowers in

spring. *Polemonium reptans* (creeping polemonium) grows to a height of 12 inches. This slowly spreading species likes a rich, moist partially shaded spot, although it is also tolerant of full sun and drier conditions. The species form has pale blue flowers, while a selection known as 'Blue Pearl' has deeper sky blue blossoms. I often like to mix the two colors together to achieve a foamy contrast of blues. *P. van-bruntiae* hails from the mountains of the East. It flowers slightly later than creeping polemonium and bears its blossoms on 18-inch stems. The color of the flowers is a deep lavender-blue against which its prominent orange stamens make a showy contrast. *P. viscosum*, a western mountain species, is very similar to *P. van-bruntiae* but has bluer flowers.

Cultural Information: Polemoniums are easy to grow in any moist, rich soil in partial shade to full sun. Cut back the flowers after bloom unless you wish to encourage them to self-sow in your garden. Space the plants 18 inches apart. Large plants can be divided in spring. Polemonium seed germinates best with a period of moist, cold stratification.

Uses: Shade or woodland garden, perennial border, groundcover.

Polygonatum biflorum
(po-lig-oh-NAY-tum   buy-FLO-rum)
Solomon's seal, Easy. ◑ ●
Origin: Eastern United States
Habitat: Woodlands
Zones: 3 to 9
Height: 1 to 3 feet
Color: White
Characteristics: Polygonatum biflorum, with its tall (1- to 3-foot), ladderlike leaves, is a common sight in the spring in eastern woodlands. It forms colonies of gracefully bent stems. Beneath these stems, the Solomon's seal bears pairs of drooping, greenish-white bells in the axils of the leaves. Even after blossoming, the leaves remain a delicate and distinctive contrast to other woodland flowers, which earns it a position of prominence in the shade garden. *P. pubescens* is a more delicate species with greener flowers, while *P. commutatum* (sometimes called *P. canaliculatum*) is a giant version that can reach heights of 5 to 7 feet. This plant forms a dramatic accent in a shady area.

Cultural Information: Solomon's seal requires a moist, humus-rich soil in partial to almost full shade. Plants should be placed fairly close together, with about 8 inches between each one. The drooping stems look best and most natural when faced in the same direc-

tion. Giant Solomon's seal can be planted further apart (at distances of 12 to 18 inches). All of the Solomon's seals should be planted in drifts as they occur in the wild. A single stem looks lonely and out of place in the garden. Plants are best divided in fall before they go dormant.

Uses: Woodland and shade gardens.

Poppy, Celandine; see *Stylophorum*

Poppy mallow; see *Callirhoe*

Poppy, wood; see *Stylophorum*

Porteranthus (syn. *Gillenia*) (por-ter-AN-thus) **bowman's root, Indian physic,** Moderate. ○ ◑
Origin: Eastern United States
Habitat: Rich woods
Zones: 4 to 8

Polygonatum biflorum

Gillenia trifoliata

Height: 3 to 4 feet
Color: White
Characteristics: Gillenia (as I prefer to call this genus because I think the name is prettier) is a little-known American genus deserving much greater attention from gardeners. The two species, *G. trifoliata* (bowman's root) and *G. stipulata* (Indian physic), both have leaves that resemble those of Japanese cut leaf maples. The bowman's root has clusters of 3 leaves, while the Indian physic has very cut leaves in clusters of 5. These plants could be grown merely for their glossy foliage, but they also bear many dainty white butterflylike flowers in late spring. The flowers of bowman's root are slightly larger and open two weeks before its cousin. On the other hand, the foliage of the Indian physic turns a deep burgundy color in the fall while that of the bowman's root changes to a duller red-brown. Both plants form giant 4-foot bushes when mature.
Cultural Information: Gillenias need a moist, humus-rich soil in full sun to light shade. In sunny positions the plants need no staking but in shadier sites they will need some support. In warmer climates they need partial shade or the foliage will burn. Plants can be grown from seed, which requires a period of moist, cold stratification in order to germinate. It takes the seedlings several years to reach maturity.
Uses: Perennial border, woodland garden.

Prairie coneflower; see *Ratibida*

Prairie dock; see *Silphium*

Prairie smoke; see *Geum*

Prickly pear; see *Opuntia*

Purple coneflower; see *Echinacea*

Pycnanthemum incanum (pick-NAN-the-mum in-KON-um) **hoary mountain mint,** Easy. ○ ◐
Origin: Eastern United States
Habitat: Upland woods
Zones: 5 to 8
Height: 2 to 3 feet
Colors: White and pink, with gray foliage
Characteristics: Pycnanthemum incanum is a gray-foliaged wildflower that becomes truly lovely in summer when its buttons of pink and white flowers are cupped from beneath by silver bracts with rose or burgundy bases. The color combination is particularly effective when grown with other perennials such as liatris that have similar rose-purple flowers. This plant spreads slowly to form a nice colony.
Cultural Information: The hoary mountain mint is easy to grow in a wide variety of situations from moderately dry to slightly moist soil in full sun to partial shade. In shadier sites plants may need staking or they can be cut back by one-third in late spring to promote branching and a more compact habit of growth. Propagate plants by division in spring or by seed, which requires a period of moist, cold stratification in order to germinate.
Uses: Perennial gardens in full sun or light shade.

Pycnanthemum
incanum *with* Liatris
aspera

Ratibida columnifera *with* Monarda didyma

Queen-of-the-prairie; see *Filipendula*

Raspberry, flowering; see *Rubus*

Ratibida (ra-TI-bi-dah) **prairie coneflower,** Easy. ○ 🌂 ❀
Origin: Western United States
Habitat: Prairies
Zones: 4 to 9
Height: 2 to 5 feet
Colors: Yellow, rust, deep red-brown

Rosa virginiana

Characteristics: The prairie coneflowers have distinctive blossoms with prominent cones or noses and sharply reflexed petals that make the flowers look like the nose of a rocket. *Ratibida columnifera* has an elongated dark cone that can reach 3 inches in length, making it a wonderful conversation piece. This plant grows to a height of 2 to 3 feet and flowers for most of the summer. The flowers of the species are yellow, while the variety *pulcherrima* has deep rusty red blossoms. *R. pinnata* has a much smaller cone, but the downward pointing petals are still very dramatic. The foliage of this plant stays low (at about 2 feet) but in midsummer it sends up tall wiry stems bearing many yellow blossoms that last all summer and into fall. The effect is very airy and light. Both plants look best when grown among ornamental grasses similar to the way they grow in their wild prairie home.
Cultural Information: Ratibidas need full sun and a rich, well-drained garden soil. The bold cones of the *Ratibida columnifera* can be used singly as an accent plant. I prefer to plant the airy *R. pinnata* in groups of three or more to create a dramatic effect in a background planting. Space plants 30 inches apart. New plants can be easily grown from seed, which requires a period of moist, cold stratification in order to germinate.
Uses: Perennial border, prairies and meadows, grass gardens.

Rattlesnake master; see *Eryngium*

Rosa (ROE-sah) **wild rose,** Easy. ○ ◑
Origin: North America
Habitat: Fields and wood edges
Zones: 4 to 9
Height: 3 to 8 feet
Color: Pink
Characteristics: The United States has a number of garden-worthy rose species that flower in the late spring and summer and bear single pink flowers. *Rosa carolina* (pasture or Carolina rose), a low plant reaching about 3 feet, can grow in moist to very dry soils. *R. virginiana* is similar, but it is usually found in dry sites and grows to a height of 6 feet. Both species are fragrant, flower in late spring to early summer and bear showy orange-red hips in fall. *R. nitida* is a dainty species native to northeastern bogs. It grows 1 to 2 feet tall, has fragrant flowers in early summer, small glossy green leaves that turn deep red in fall and red hips as well. *R. setigera* is a tall-growing prairie rose particularly prized for its large flowers and late bloom season in July and August. Because of its tall habit of growth, large flowers, summer bloom and hardiness, it was used to breed many climbers and ramblers at the turn of the century such as the popular 'American Pillar' in 1902.
Cultural Information: The native roses do their best in full sun in a humus-rich site that is moist but well drained. *Rosa nitida* will tolerate very moist conditions, while *R. carolina* is a vigorous suckering groundcover for dry soils. Prune out dead wood in the spring. Little spraying is necessary because the species roses are fairly disease free.
Uses: Shrub border, perennial garden, groundcover.

Rose mallow; see *Hibiscus*

Rose, wild; see *Rosa*

Rubus (RUE-bus) **flowering raspberry, thimbleberry,** Easy. ◑ ● ✿
Origin: North America
Habitat: Woods
Zones: 3 to 8
Height: 4 to 5 feet
Colors: Lavender-pink, white
Characteristics: The flowering

Rubus odoratus

raspberries are a little-known group of wildflowers that flower all summer. They have bold, light green maple-shaped leaves that provide a nice contrast in a shady garden. *Rubus odoratus*, the eastern species, has lavender-pink flowers; *R. parviflorus*, the western version, looks almost identical but bears white flowers. Plants grow to a height of 5 feet and will send up suckers all around the parent plant to form a colony 6 feet or more in spread. Flowering raspberries are useful for making that often difficult transition from wild woodland to more cultivated garden. Because they are vigorous and ornamental, they are perfect for those in-between locations.

Cultural Information: Both species like a little bit of filtered light. You find them growing at wood edges in the wild. Given a humus-rich soil, they are quite tolerant of both moist and fairly dry conditions. Stems of flowering raspberries are woody with peeling brown bark. The plants send up many new shoots each spring and flowers appear on old and new stems alike. Plants are easily divided in spring to form new colonies.

Uses: Shade and woodland gardens, naturalizing.

Rudbeckia (rude-BECK-ee-ah) coneflower, black-eyed Susan, Easy. ○ 🌡 ❀

Origin: North America
Habitat: Meadows and prairies
Zones: 3 to 9
Height: 2 to 6 feet
Colors: Yellow, orange
Characteristics: Rudbeckia is a North American genus with

some very ornamental species. The perennial *Rudbeckia fulgida* 'Goldsturm', is one of the most popular wildflowers. This prairie black-eyed Susan flowers all summer long with brilliant orange-yellow blossoms and deep brown cones on 2-foot stems. *R. laciniata* has drooping yellow petals with a green cone. It also flowers in summer, but it grows to 5 to 6 feet. 'Golden Glow', a double form of this plant, was first introduced in 1894 and is still found growing around many older homes. *R. nitida* 'Herbstsonne' is similar to *R. laciniata* but has larger flowers with drooping yellow petals. Growing to a height of 4 to 5 feet, this plant is a showy addition to the late summer garden. *R. triloba* flowers in late summer and autumn with smaller orange-yellow petals surrounding a dark cone on 3-foot stems. It is simply covered with blossoms for several months and makes a stunning show. *R. maxima* is rapidly becoming popular for its bold gray leaves and yellow flowers with an elongated brown nose. When in flower, this plant reaches a towering height of 6 feet or more.

Cultural Information: All of the rudbeckias prefer a rich, moist soil in full sun. Most plants should be cut back after flowering. *Rudbeckia fulgida* 'Goldsturm', however, has seed pods that often remain ornamental through the winter, so it can be cut back in early spring. Rudbeckias can be grown from seed, which germinates best after a period of moist, cold stratification. The special cultivars should be increased by di-

vision in spring or fall.
Uses: Perennial gardens, meadows, naturalizing, cut flower.

Rue, tall meadow; see ***Thalictrum***

Sage, mealy-cup; see ***Salvia***

Sage, white; see ***Artemisia***

Salvia farinacea (SAL-vee-ah far-in-EH-see-ah) mealy-cup sage, Easy. ○ ◑ 🌡 ❀

Origin: Southwestern United States
Habitat: Meadows
Zones: 7 to 10
Height: 1 to 3 feet
Colors: Blue, white
Characteristics: *Salvia farinacea* is a tender perennial hardy only in warmer climates. However, it bears such a profusion of spikes of purple-blue flowers for such a long season (from late spring through frost), that it is now commonly grown as an annual. Mealy-cup sage blends easily in perennial gardens and provides a splash of blue for most of the season. 'Victoria Blue' is a low-growing selection that reaches only 18 inches in height. 'Silver White' is a dwarf white-flowered form. The flowers hold their color well when dried for use as an everlasting in bouquets and wreaths.

Cultural Information: *Salvia farinacea* is easily grown in full sun to light shade in a moderately moist, humus-rich soil. It also makes a very good container or window box plant due to its long season of bloom. Plants are easily grown from seed and should be started indoors 8 to 10 weeks before the

Rudbeckia fulgida
'Goldsturm'

Salvia farinacea
'Victoria Blue'

Sanguinaria canadensis

Sanguinaria canadensis *var.* multiplex

last frost date to gain a long season of bloom.
Uses: Perennial and annual borders, planters, cut flower and dried flower.

Sanguinaria canadensis (san-gwi-NAIR-ee-ah can-ah-DEN-sis) **bloodroot,** Easy. ◑ ●

Origin: Eastern North America
Habitat: Woodlands
Zones: 3 to 9
Height: 4 to 6 inches
Color: White
Characteristics: Sanguinaria canadensis is one of the earliest flowers of spring. It is com-

monly found in the wild growing in great drifts. The single, white 2-inch blossoms do not last longer than a day or two. There are always new flowers opening, however, so the season of bloom often lasts for a couple of weeks providing the days stay cool. After the flowers have passed, scalloped gray-green leaves open to form a very beautiful groundcover. In moist soil the leaves will remain effective for the entire summer, but plants will go dormant if conditions become dry. The common name of bloodroot comes from the bright orange-red sap of the plant, which is particularly noticeable when its root is broken. There is a double form of bloodroot known as var. *multiplex*, which has many white petals and looks like a waterlily. This beauty deserves a finer name than "multiplex"; something like 'Woodland Waterlily' would be more appropriate.
Cultural Information: Sanguinaria does best in a humus-rich soil in partial shade with a good supply of moisture in spring. It withstands drought in summer, but the plant will go dormant under these conditions. When happy, bloodroot quickly forms a nice colony and will even self-sow to nearby spots in the garden. The easiest way to propagate bloodroot is to divide it in the spring. Make sure each piece of root has a leaf attached to it and replant it at the same depth (approximately 2 inches), at which it was originally growing. Plants should be spaced anywhere from 6 to 12 inches apart. They look best when

planted in groups instead of singly.
Uses: Shade and woodland gardens, groundcover.

Sanguisorba canadensis (san-gwi-SOR-bah can-ah-DEN-sis) **Canadian burnet,** Easy. ○ ◑ ✿

Origin: Eastern United States
Habitat: Swamps
Zones: 3 to 8
Height: 5 to 6 feet
Color: White
Characteristics: Canadian burnet is a bold plant for the middle or background of a garden. It has large, pinnately cut leaves that are 2½ feet high and elongated, bottlebrushlike white flowers that reach a height of 5 to 6 feet. It begins blooming in late summer and continues for much of the fall. I have never had to stake this plant; it stands well on its own. The creamy white blossoms are beautiful when backlit by the low sunlight of autumn.

Sanguisorba canadensis

Cultural Information: In the wild, Canadian burnet inhabits very wet sites, but in cultivation it is easily satisfied with the average moisture requirements of most perennials. For the most robust growth, give it a soil rich in organic matter. This is a large grower, so space young plants 3 to 4 feet apart. Propagate it by division in spring.

Uses: Perennial border, meadows.

Saxifraga pensylvanica (sax-i-FROG-ah pen-sil-VAN-i-kah) **swamp saxifrage,** Easy. ○ ◐

Origin: Eastern United States.
Habitat: Swamps, wet meadows
Zones: 4 to 8
Height: 1 to 3 feet
Color: White
Characteristics: *Saxifraga pensylvanica* makes a terrific addition to a moist garden in full sun to light shade. It has hairy, straplike basal leaves and sends up thick stalks of greenish-white flowers in spring that can reach a height of 3 feet. While the flowers are not showy, the plant as a whole creates a dramatic effect because of its strong vertical and horizontal lines.

Cultural Information: The swamp saxifrage is easily grown in full sun to light shade in a rich, moist soil. In hotter climates it will need partial shade and fairly moist conditions. Plants should be spaced 2½ to 3 feet apart. *Saxifraga pensylvanica* can be divided in spring or it can be grown from seed, which requires a period of moist, cold stratification in order to germinate.

Uses: Pond side planting, damp garden, perennial border.

Saxifrage, swamp; see *Saxifraga*

Scutellaria (scoo-tell-AIR-ee-ah) **skullcap,** Moderate. ○ ◐

Origin: Eastern United States
Habitat: Fields and wood edges
Zones: 5 to 9
Height: 2 to 4 feet
Color: Blue
Characteristics: Scutellaria has intriguing hooded blue flowers in showy clusters that give a foamy appearance when massed. There are several species that bear similar flowers but bloom at different times during the season. *Scutellaria serrata* (showy skullcap) is a 2-foot plant that prefers a slightly shaded location and flowers in midspring. *S. integrifolia* (hyssop skullcap) grows well in sun or light shade, reaches a height of 18 inches and blooms in late spring and early summer. *S. incana* (downy skullcap) produces its crop of showy blue flowers in late summer and fall.

It reaches a height of 3 to 4 feet and grows well in full sun or light shade.

Cultural Information: All of the scutellarias appreciate a humus-rich soil in light shade to full sun. In full sun the leaves often take on a pretty burgundy tinge. Don't deadhead because the seed pods are quite ornamental. Space the lower growing skullcaps 18 inches apart and the taller growing species 3 feet apart. Scutellarias can be grown from seed, which requires a moist, cold period of stratification in order to germinate.

Uses: Perennial border, shade and woodland gardens.

Saxifraga pensylvanica

Sedum ternatum (SEE-dum ter-NAH-tum) **woodland stonecrop,** Easy. ○ ◐

Origin: Eastern United States
Habitat: Rocky woodlands
Zones: 4 to 8
Height: 3 to 6 inches
Color: White
Characteristics: Unlike most sedums, which are drought-

Sedum ternatum

Scutellaria serrata *with* Lonicera sempervirens *var.* flava

tolerant sun lovers, the woodland stonecrop occurs naturally in moist, shaded rocky sites in the eastern United States. This noninvasive sedum has low rosettes of fleshy leaves that slowly creep along the ground. In spring, the woodland stonecrop is covered with many starry white flowers that give the appearance of foam on the forest floor. The evergreen foliage often takes on a deep red tint during the winter, which makes this plant attractive for all four seasons.

Cultural Information: Sedum *ternatum* is easily grown in any partially shaded site. It is happiest when planted in a humus-rich soil that remains a bit moist all season long. Space new plants 6 to 8 inches apart. The easiest way to propagate this plant is to divide it in spring or autumn.

Uses: Shade or woodland gardens, groundcover.

Shooting star; see Dodecatheon

Silene (sy-LEE-nee) **pink,** Moderate. ○ ◑
Origin: North America
Habitat: Rocky woodlands
Zones: 5 to 8
Height: 6 inches to 2 feet
Colors: Pink, red
Characteristics: The native pinks bear showy, 5-petaled flowers in spring. *Silene caroliniana,* an eastern native, has gray-green foliage that grows in a low 6- to 8-inch mound and is covered with soft pink blossoms. The following pinks are notable for their bright red flowers: *S. virginica* (the eastern fire pink); *S. californica* (the California Indian pink), which is native to California and Oregon; and *S. mexicana* (the Mexican pink), which can be found growing wild in the Southwest. The flowers of these 18-inch plants stand out because red is an unusual spring color.

Cultural Information: All of the silenes will grow in full sun to light shade. They all occur on rocky woodland sites in the wild and prefer a similar well-drained but humus-rich soil in the garden. The silenes are not strong competitors, so do not plant them near other plants that are very vigorous or next to ones that are prone to flop on top of them. Plant in groups of three or more for best effect and space individuals 12 to 18 inches apart. Plants can be grown from seed, which requires a period of moist, cold stratification in order to germinate.

Uses: Perennial border, rock garden.

Silphium (SIL-fee-um) **cup-plant, compass plant, prairie dock,** Easy. ○ ✿
Origin: Central United States
Habitat: Tall grass prairies
Zones: 3 to 9
Height: 5 to 9 feet
Color: Yellow
Characteristics: Silphium is yet another genus found only in North America. All silphium bear clear yellow 3-inch sunflowers in summer. Great vari-

Silene virginica

Silphium perfoliatum

ety in foliage and habit of growth separate the species from each other and make them useful garden plants. *Silphium perfoliatum* begins flowering in early summer. It is a big and vigorous grower with large leaves that "cup" the stems, hence its common name of cup-plant. It is said that Indians and early settlers drank the dew or rainwater that collected in these natural cups. *S. laciniatum* has large, deeply incised, mule-ear type leaves that can reach a height of 1½ to 2 feet. The slightly grayish leaves with their distinctive lobes and showy yellow flowers that rise on a long stalk to a height of 6 to 9 feet in mid- to late summer earn this plant a place in the perennial garden. Its common name of compass plant comes from the fact that the leaves orient themselves in a north-south direction. *S. terebinthinaceum* (prairie dock), has 2-foot-long leaves that are more rounded and not lobed like the compass plant. These leaves make a fine contrast in a perennial border or ornamental grass garden. Prairie dock also sends up its flowers on very tall (6- to 8-foot) stalks in mid- to late summer. Birds love the seed of all of the silphiums.
Cultural Information: Silphiums require full sun and rich, moist soils. The compass plants and prairie dock take several years to reach maturity. Space the fast-growing cup-plant 5 to 6 feet apart and the other two species 3 to 4 feet apart. You might want to fill the extra space with annuals in the first couple of years until the compass plant and the prairie dock

are full grown. Silphiums have deep taproots so the best method of propagation is seed. Seed germinates readily after a period of moist, cold stratification.
Uses: Prairie plantings, perennial borders, pond side areas, interplanted with ornamental grasses.

Skullcap; see *Scutellaria*

Smilacina racemosa
(smy-lah-SEE-nah ra-seh-MOE-sah)
false Solomon's seal, Solomon's plume, Easy. ◑ ●
Origin: North America
Habitat: Rich woods
Zones: 3 to 7
Height: 2 to 3 feet
Color: White
Characteristics: Smilacina racemosa has similar ladderlike foliage to the true Solomon's seal, *Polygonatum biflorum,* but its flowers are entirely different. The blossoms of the false Solomon's seal are located at the apex of the stem, not at the leaf axils. The many tiny white flowers combine to form a showy white plume in spring. In fall it produces red berries that appear to be splashed with gold dust. *S. racemosa* is a much showier garden plant than the polygonatums and is found growing in rich, moist woods across most of the United States. *S. stellata* (starry Solomon's seal) is another species that is found in the wild from coast to coast. It has more succulent leaves and a less showy inflorescence, but its fruit turns an attractive deep red in fall. Found in a variety of habitats from moist woods to wet sandy sites to exposed dunes, the starry Solomon's

Smilacina racemosa

seal is a very adaptable plant for a variety of garden sites.
Cultural Information: The false Solomon's seals do their best in a rich, moist, organic soil in partial shade. They should be planted in masses, as they are found in the wild. For a natural and graceful effect make sure you point all of the stems in the same direction. Space individual rhizomes 4 to 6 inches apart and space a group of rhizomes 18 inches away from other plants. The easiest way to propagate smilacina is by division in spring.
Uses: Shade or woodland garden, naturalizing.

Snakeroot; see ***Eupatorium***

Sneezeweed; see ***Helenium***

Soapweed; see ***Yucca***

Solidago (sol-i-DAY-go) **goldenrod,** Easy. ○ ◑ ⬤
Origin: North America
Habitat: Meadows and woods
Zones: 3 to 9

Solidago canadensis
'Golden Baby'

Height: 2 to 5 feet
Color: Yellow
Characteristics: The showy yellow blossoms of goldenrods have a bad name in the United States due to the misconception that they cause hay fever. In fact, it is the less showy wind-pollinated ragweed that blooms at the same time that is the real culprit. However, if a gardener realizes this and decides to try out some roadside species of goldenrod, chances are the transplanted beauty will quickly overrun the garden. Many of the 72 native species of goldenrod are better left in the wild, but a number of the solidagos do make fine garden specimens. *Solidago canadensis* 'Golden Baby' is a low-growing form that reaches only 2 feet in height and bears gracefully nodding, showy golden plumes in midsummer. *S. speciosa* (showy goldenrod) has great loose yellow cones of flowers in late summer and grows to be 4 to 5 feet tall. *S. sempervirens* (seaside goldenrod) is a personal favorite of mine. It has more succulent leaves than most other goldenrods and is adapted to growing in harsh seaside conditions, although it is equally at home in more standard garden soils. Seaside goldenrod flowers late in the season with tight plumes of bright clear yellow that provide a wonderful contrast to the reds and oranges of autumn. It grows to be 3 to 5 feet tall depending upon how much water it receives.
Cultural Information: All of these goldenrods need to be grown in full sun. *Solidago canadensis* does best in moder-

ately moist soil while *S. speciosa* and *S. sempervirens* are tolerant of average to dry soils. Turn in some compost before planting and space plants 2 feet apart for the dwarf-growing 'Golden Baby', 4 feet apart for *speciosa* which is a wide grower, and 3 feet apart for *S. sempervirens*, which tends to have more of an upright habit of growth. Goldenrods are easily divided in spring or fall. The species will also come true from seed, which requires a period of moist, cold stratification in order to germinate.
Uses: Perennial garden, meadow, cut flower.

Solomon's plume; see ***Smilacina***

Solomon's seal; see ***Polygonatum***

Solomon's seal, false; see ***Smilacina***

Spanish bayonet; see ***Yucca***

Spiderwort; see ***Tradescantia***

Spikenard; see ***Aralia***

Spurge, Allegheny; see ***Pachysandra***

Stoke's aster; see ***Stokesia***

Stokesia laevis (stoe-KEE-zee-ah LAY-vis) **Stoke's aster,** Easy. ○ ◑ ☀ 🔔 ✿
Origin: Southeastern United States
Habitat: Moist pinelands
Zones: 5 to 9
Height: 1 to 2 feet
Colors: Blue, white
Characteristics: Throughout most of the summer, the clear blue cornflowerlike blossoms of the stokesia emerge from evergreen basal rosettes. Compact growth (of approximately 18 inches) and many big happy blue flowers have made this wildflower a very popular garden plant. *Stokesia laevis* is now available in some new and improved forms. 'Blue Danube'

Stokesia laevis

has large, deep blue flowers, 'Silver Moon' is a white-flowered selection and 'Klaus Jelitto' has very large pale blue blossoms.

Cultural Information: Stokesia laevis likes a fertile, moist but well-drained soil in full sun to partial shade. Keep the plants deadheaded to prolong the period of bloom. In Zone 5, where the plants are not fully ever-green, they may need a winter mulch. Space plants 12 to 18 inches apart. Propagate the named cultivars by division in spring. The species can be grown from seed, which needs a period of moist, cold stratification in order to germinate.

Uses: Perennial garden, ground-cover, cut flower.

Stonecrop, woodland; see *Sedum*

Strawberry, barren; see *Waldsteinia*

Stylophorum diphyllum
(sty-lah-FOR-um die-FILL-um) **wood poppy, celandine poppy,** Easy. ◐ ● ✿

Origin: Central and southeastern United States
Habitat: Moist woodlands
Zones: 4 to 9
Height: 12 to 30 inches
Color: Yellow
Characteristics: Why isn't the wood poppy more commonly grown? It is one of the showiest of the spring wildflowers and it is very easy to cultivate. It begins flowering in early spring and keeps going for many weeks. The 2-inch shiny yellow flowers make a beautiful contrast to the many blue, white and lavender blossoms of

spring. It is a natural for combining with the woodland phloxes. Don't confuse this plant with the weedy false celandine, which is a common pest; this wood poppy has much larger and showier flowers and more architectural leaves. After flowering, the wood poppy produces intriguing drooping seed pods that are covered with small bristles. In drier woodland sites, the wood poppy will go dormant in midsummer. In moist to average soils the plant will remain up through the fall.

Cultural Information: Grow *Stylophorum diphyllum* in a moist, humus-rich soil in partial shade. It is wonderful planted in drifts and also when allowed to self-sow among other perennials and ferns. Unwanted seedlings are easily pulled out. The best way to propagate this plant is to allow it to self-sow and then move the young seedlings to their new home in spring. Space plants 18 inches apart.

Uses: Shade and woodland gardens, naturalizing.

Sundrops; see *Oenothera*

Sunflower; see *Helianthus*

Sunflower, ox-eye; see *Heliopsis*

Swamp saxifrage; see *Saxifraga*

Tall meadow-rue; see *Thalictrum*

Tellima; see *Mitella*

Stylophorum diphyllum

Thalictrum polygamum *with* Digitalis purpurea

Thalictrum polygamum
(thal-IK-trum pol-IG-ah-mum) **tall meadow-rue,** Easy. ◐

Origin: Eastern North America
Habitat: Swamps and stream sides
Zones: 3 to 8
Height: 5 to 7 feet
Color: White
Characteristics: Majestic height, delicately lobed gray-green foliage, and a cloud of dainty white flowers in late spring and early summer describe this easily cultivated but little-known thalictrum. The fact that

it is so commonly seen in moist sites in the wild could explain why it has been overlooked as a garden plant. Those who grow meadow-rue fall in love with it. Meadow-rue is a perfect background plant for the shade garden. Its delicate leaves provide a light textural contrast with other heavier foliaged plants.

Cultural Information: Thalictrum polygamum should be grown in a moist, humus-rich site in partial shade. In very rich soils the plants will need a little discreet support. Space plants 2½ feet apart. New plants can be grown from seed, which requires a period of moist, cold stratification in order to germinate.

Uses: Shade, woodland and damp gardens.

Thermopsis caroliniana

Thermopsis (ther-MOP-sis) false lupine, Moderate. ○ ◑ ◐ ❋

Origin: North America
Habitat: Dry woods and meadows
Zones: 3 to 9
Height: 18 inches to 4 feet
Color: Yellow
Characteristics: Thermopsis bear many showy yellow lupine-like flowers above three divided green leaves. *Thermopsis caroliniana,* which is native to the Southeast, grows to a height of 4 feet. *T. montana* is a very similar western relative that grows only 18 to 24 inches tall. Both species are undemanding perennials that add a welcome splash of clear yellow blossoms to the spring garden. Thermopsis and the blue baptisias make good substitutes for lupines in hot, humid climates

where true lupines are often difficult to grow.

Cultural Information: Thermopsis should be grown in full sun in the North and in partial shade in hotter climates. They like a rich but well-drained soil. Plants are best propagated by seed, which should be soaked in warm water for 24 hours before sowing. Young plants resent having their roots disturbed, so sow each seed singly in an individual pot.

Uses: Perennial garden and meadows.

Thimbleberry; see *Rubus*

Tiarella (tee-ah-REL-lah) foamflower, Easy. ◑ ● ❚

Origin: North America
Habitat: Rich woods
Zones: 3 to 8
Height: 6 to 12 inches
Colors: White to pale pink
Characteristics: The foamflowers are an essential choice for any shady garden. They have pretty heart-shaped leaves and bear so many spikes of dainty white flowers that they give an effect of foam on the woodland floor when in bloom. The most commonly available species is *Tiarella cordifolia,* which is native to the eastern United States. It is easily distinguished by its long runners and the creeping habit of the 6-inch plant. The creeping *T. cordifolia* makes a fast-growing woodland groundcover that is not invasive and is also tolerant of fairly dry shady sites. *T. wherryi* is a more southern species that differs from *T. cordifolia* primarily by its non-creeping, clump-forming habit of growth. Some nurseries sell

this plant as *Tiarella cordifolia* var. *collina* or *T. collina.* It is a larger growing plant that can reach a height of 1 foot when in flower. The individual flowers are also a bit showier and tend to have a pink tinge to them. There is considerable variation to be found in both species and recently growers have been having fun introducing all sorts of new varieties with different shaped leaves. For example, 'Slickrock' has deeply cut maple-shaped leaves, pinkish flowers and a creeping habit of growth and 'Oakleaf' has deeply lobed leaves and is a clump former.

Cultural Information: Tiarellas will grow their fastest in a moist, humus-rich soil in partial shade; however, they are tolerant of fairly dense shade and drier conditions. Under these conditions they will grow more slowly. Plants can be increased by a variety of means. Tiarellas can be divided in spring and are easily grown from seed, which requires a period of moist, cold stratification

Tiarella cordifolia *with* Phlox divaricata

in order to germinate. In the case of the stoloniferous *Tiarella cordifolia*, the stems, which root along the ground, can be carefully cut from the mother plant and dug up and moved in spring. Space Tiarellas 2 feet apart.

Uses: Shade or woodland gardens, groundcover.

Tickseed; see ***Coreopsis***

Tradescantia (tra-des-KAN-tee-ah) **spiderwort,** Easy. ○ ◑ ▮ ❀

Origin: Throughout the United States
Habitat: Wood edges, prairies
Zones: 5 to 9
Height: 8 to 30 inches
Colors: Blue, purple, pink, red, white
Characteristics: Spiderworts have succulent grassy foliage and tight clusters of three-petaled blossoms. Each flower lasts only a day, but new ones keep opening and the plants are in bloom for several months in late spring through summer. The most commonly available tradescantias are hybrids of several native species: *Tradescantia ohiensis*, *T. subaspera* and *T. virginiana*. Known as *T. × andersoniana*, these hybrids have larger flowers than the species, grow to be about 2 feet tall and come in a wide variety of colors. 'Red Cloud' is a deep magenta pink, 'Zwanenburg Blue' is a clear blue and 'Snowcap' is a clear white. All of these hybrids make showy plants for the perennial garden. *T. hirsuticaulis* is a southeastern native that grows only 8 to 10 inches tall and has intense violet-blue blossoms in late

spring. During the summer it goes dormant and then the foliage grows back in fall.
Cultural Information: Tradescantias bloom best when grown in full sun. In richer soils, the plants tend to get large and sprawl in midsummer. If this happens, it is often advisable to cut back the foliage and allow it to grow again to a lower and tidier height. Sometimes after such a pruning you will be rewarded with flowers again in fall. Space plants 2½ feet apart. Spiderworts are easily divided in spring or fall. They also self-sow in the garden but the selected color forms will produce seedlings in a range of colors.
Uses: Perennial garden, naturalizing, rock gardens (for the smaller species).

Turtlehead; see ***Chelone***

Uvularia (oo-vah-LAI-ree-ah) **merrybells, bellwort,** Moderate. ◑
Origin: Eastern United States
Habitat: Rich woods
Zones: 3 to 8
Height: 6 to 24 inches
Color: Yellow
Characteristics: Uvularia are graceful woodlanders with clear yellow nodding blossoms in spring. The showiest of the 5 native species is *Uvularia grandiflora* (large-flowered merrybells). It begins blooming almost as soon as the foliage emerges from the ground. As the stems grow, the flowers are carried upward to a height of almost 2 feet. During the summer, the slightly grayish foliage remains a good contrast to other greener leaves. *U. perfoliata* (perfoliate merrybells) has

Tradescantia virginiana

Uvularia grandiflora *with* Tiarella cordifolia *and* Stylophorum diphyllum

smaller yet still pretty flowers and grows to a height of only 8 to 12 inches.
Cultural Information: Uvularias like a situation similar to that of their woodland homes. They prefer a rich, moist site in partial shade. For the delicate beauty of the merrybells to be effective, they should be planted in groups of three or more, spaced 8 inches apart. Uvularias can be divided in spring or fall. They seem to respond well to division and often return to the

size of the original planting within a year.

Uses: Shade or woodland garden.

Valerian, creeping; see ***Polemonium***

Vancouveria hexandra (van-koo-VER-ee-ah hex-AN-drah) **vancouveria, inside-out flower,** Easy. ◐ ●
Origin: Northwestern United States
Habitat: Forests
Zones: 5 to 8
Height: 8 to 12 inches
Color: White

Vancouveria hexandra

Characteristics: With delicate foliage similar to that of the Japanese epimediums, *Vancouveria hexandra* lends a light and airy appearance to the garden. It bears small white flowers in late spring that, while not showy, are interesting. The sharply reflexed flower petals give rise to the common name of inside-out flower. This northwestern forest dweller has a creeping rootstock that forms a dense, 10-inch-tall groundcover for shady sites.

Cultural Information: Grow vancouveria in a rich, moist soil in a shady site. Allow it plenty of room to spread into a great drift. Space plants 15 inches apart. The easiest way to propagate vancouveria is by division in spring.

Uses: Shade or woodland garden, groundcover.

Verbena (ver-BEE-nah) **verbena, vervain,** Easy. ○ 🮑 ❀
Origin: Throughout the United States
Habitat: Moist and dry fields
Zones: 3 to 10

Height: 6 inches to 5 feet
Colors: Blue, purple, rose, white
Characteristics: Many of the pretty verbenas we see growing along roadsides are not natives but are naturalized species. Plants such as *Verbena bonariensis* and *V. tenuisecta* make good garden plants in the warmer sections of the country, but are actually native to South America. *V. hastata* (wild vervain) is the most widespread of the native verbenas. Commonly found in moist meadows across the United States, it blooms in late summer with spikes of lavender-blue that reach a height of 4 to 5 feet. This is a pretty flower for the late summer perennial border. It looks best when combined with grasses and some of the other moisture-loving wildflowers such as Joe Pye weed and New York ironweed. *V. canadensis,* a southeastern native, bears the familiar umbels of flowers seen in the annual verbenas. The species form is a fairly vigorous

colonizer in a sandy, well-drained site and is hardy to Zone 6. It reaches a height of only 8 inches and blooms with vivid hot pink flowers from spring through fall. There are other color forms available including deep purple, white and red-violet.

Cultural Information: Grow *Verbena hastata* in a rich, slightly moist organic soil in full sun. The lower leaves of this plant often look unsightly, so plan to place a perennial that has good foliage and a medium tall growth habit in front of it. Space plants 2 feet apart. *V. canadensis* needs a very sunny site with good drainage, especially in winter. Place plants about 2 feet apart and allow them to grow together as a groundcover. *V. hastata* can be grown from seed, which requires a period of moist, cold stratification in order to germinate. *V. canadensis* can be increased by divisions in spring.

Uses: Perennial gardens, meadows, rock gardens.

Verbena hastata

*Vernonia **noveboracensis*** (ver-NO-nee-ah no-ve-bor-ah-SEN-sis) **ironweed,** Easy. ○
Origin: Eastern United States
Habitat: Wet meadows
Zones: 4 to 9
Height: 5 to 7 feet
Color: Magenta-purple
Characteristics: Ironweed is a robust 6- to 7-foot plant that bears great flat clusters of deep magenta-purple blossoms in late summer and autumn. While scything a meadow of these plants one fall I learned why they bear the common name of ironweed. Every time I encountered the stems of the vernonia, the scythe came to an abrupt halt and my body vibrated like a cartoon character. Stem strength aside, vernonia makes a showy plant for the back of the late summer perennial border. It combines particularly well with the larger ornamental grasses and Joe Pye weeds. I don't cut back the plant until spring because I enjoy looking at the tawny seedheads during the winter.
Cultural Information: Ironweed is easily grown in any sunny garden with moist to average soil. In the wild it is often found in very moist sites and thus is a good choice for a similar damp spot in the garden or around a pond. I have not found it necessary to stake the stems because they are strong enough to support the blossoms on their own. Sometimes I have cut back the plant by one-third to one-half in late spring to induce more flowers at a lower height. Space plants 3 to 4 feet apart. Plants can be grown from seed, which requires a moist, cold period of stratification in order to germinate.
Uses: Perennial border, meadow.

*Veronicastrum **virginicum*** (ve-ron-i-KAS-trum vir-JIN-i-kum) **Culver's-root,** Easy. ○ ◑
Origin: Eastern United States
Habitat: Moist meadows
Zones: 4 to 8
Height: 4 to 5 feet
Colors: White, pale pink
Characteristics: Whorls of shiny green leaves arranged in horizontal tiers and showy spikes of white flowers make *Veronicastrum virginicum* a dramatic asset to any perennial border. Culver's-root grows to a height of 4 to 5 feet and flowers in mid- to late summer. The variety *roseum* has pale pink flowers and the variety *alba* has very clear white blossoms.
Cultural Information: In the wild, veronicastrum is found in moist meadows and wood edges. In the garden, it prefers a rich organic soil and moist to average conditions. If it is grown in partial shade the plant will require staking. In full sun the plant stands on its own and flowers more freely. Space plants 3 feet apart. Division in spring is the easiest method of propagation.
Uses: Perennial border, moist meadow.

Vervain; see *Verbena*

Viola (vee-OH-lah) **violet,** Easy. ◑ ● ✿
Origin: Throughout the United States
Habitat: Woods, fields
Zones: 3 to 9
Height: 6 to 12 inches

Vernonia noveboracensis

Veronicastrum virginicum

Viola labradorica

Colors: White, blue, yellow

Characteristics: Violets are familiar and happy signs of spring. They are found growing in the wild practically throughout the world. The United States is no exception, and has some very pretty native species. *Viola labradorica* (Labrador violet) is native to northern North America, but grows well as far south as Zone 8. Its beauty lies in deep green, purple-tinged leaves and lavender flowers, which contrast nicely with the darker foliage. The Labrador violet spreads slowly to form a very beautiful groundcover in the woodland garden or under shrubs. *V. canadensis* (Canadian violet) is native to woodlands across the country. It is much taller than most violets, reaching a height of 1 foot or more. In spring it bears white flowers in the axils of the leaves. This violet is a clump former and not invasive in the garden, although it will self-sow when happily established. *V. pedata* (birdsfoot violet) is unusual because it is found not in shady moist woods, but rather in sandy dry fields and wood edges. It has distinctively cut leaves reminiscent of a bird's foot and very large and showy blue flowers in spring.

Cultural Information: Most violets prefer a rich, slightly moist, shady site in the garden. An exception is *Viola pedata*, which requires a sandy, well-drained soil in sun to partial shade. There are a great many pretty, native violets that deserve a place in the wildflower or shade garden. If you are experimenting with some of the

Waldsteinia fragarioides

species native to your area, however, be careful to observe the plant's habit of growth before moving it to your garden. You don't want to introduce a weed that is hard to control. Space most violets 12 inches apart. Propagate plants by division in fall or spring.

Uses: Shade or woodland garden, rock garden, groundcover.

Violet; see *Viola*

Virginia bluebells; see *Mertensia*

Waldsteinia fragarioides (wald-STINE-ee-ah fray-gar-ee-OI-deez) **barren strawberry,** Easy. ○ ◑

Origin: Eastern United States

Habitat: Woods

Zones: 4 to 7

Height: 4 to 8 inches

Color: Yellow

Characteristics: Waldsteinia has dark green, strawberrylike leaves and small yellow flowers in spring. While never smothered in flowers, the barren strawberry is still a beautiful groundcover because of its

tight habit of growth and glossy ornamental leaves that remain evergreen in shadier and warmer climates. In Zone 5, in full sun, it is evergreen until about midwinter. Waldsteinia makes a terrific groundcover that slowly creeps along the ground and is effective in woodland gardens or under shrubs.

Cultural Information: Waldsteinia should be grown in a rich, moist soil in full sun to light shade. The warmer the climate, the more shade it needs. Space plants 12 inches apart. Propagate the barren strawberry by division in spring.

Uses: Shade or woodland garden, groundcover for sun or shade.

Wandflower; see *Gaura*

White sage; see *Artemisia*

Wild bergamot; see *Monarda*

Wild bleeding-heart; see *Dicentra*

Wild geranium; see *Geranium*

Wild ginger; see *Asarum*

Wild indigo; see *Baptisia*

Wild rose; see *Rosa*

Wild senna; see *Cassia*

Willow amsonia; see *Amsonia*

Wine cups; see *Callirhoe*

Wood poppy; see *Stylophorum*

Woodland stonecrop; see *Sedum*

Yucca (YUCK-ah) **yucca, Spanish bayonet, soapweed,** Easy. ○
Origin: Throughout the United States
Habitat: Sandy, dry soil
Zones: 4 to 10
Height: 4 to 6 feet
Color: White
Characteristics: The distinctive upright, pointed leaves of the yucca make a vivid contrast to other perennial wildflowers. Even if they did not flower, it would be worth including yuccas in a planting purely for their architectural foliage. They do blossom, however, in summer with tall, waxy, bell-like flowers that reach a height of 6 feet or more. *Yucca filamentosa,* (Spanish bayonet or Adam's needle) is native to the Southeast. It has broad, sword-shaped leaves often with attractive fraying silver hairs at the leaf edges. *Y. glauca,* soapweed, has much narrower pointed

leaves and is native to the central United States. *Y. whipplei* (our Lord's candle) is the giant of the group. It bears great panicles of purple-tinged blossoms to heights of 6 to 12 feet. It is native to southern California and hardy to Zone 8.
Cultural Information: Yuccas need a sunny site and sandy, well-drained soil. Plants slowly increase by forming offshoots. The basal rosettes die after they flower, but there are always more rosettes in the clump to fill in and keep the plant looking good. I cut back the flower stalks after blooming because I don't think they're attractive once the flowers are gone. Space plants 4 feet apart. Propagate yuccas by division in spring; but be forewarned that they can be tough to dig up and you will need an ax or saw to cut the rosettes apart.
Uses: Perennial gardens, xeriscapes, seaside plantings.

Zauschneria californica (zaush-NER-ee-ah ka-li-FOR-ni-kah) **California fuchsia,** Moderate. ○ ◑ ◒ ✳ ❀
Origin: California
Habitat: Dry, gravelly sites
Zones: 7 to 10
Height: 1 to 2 feet
Colors: Red, pink
Characteristics: *Zauschneria californica* bears many tubular scarlet flowers in late summer and fall that are attractive to hummingbirds. It can be a rampant grower, but when placed correctly, it becomes a lovely groundcover for dry sunny sites. In warm climates the foliage remains evergreen all winter. Selections of the species available from nurseries

Yucca glauca

include 'Glasnevin' (or 'Dublin' as it is sometimes called), which grows to a height of 8 inches and has scarlet flowers, the less invasive 'Arizonica' also has scarlet blossoms but grows to 2 feet, and 'Solidarity Pink,' which has gray leaves and soft pink flowers.
Cultural Information: Zauschneria should be grown in a lean, well-drained soil in full sun to light shade. Good drainage is especially important in climates with very wet winters. If the plants become leggy they can be pinched to encourage branching. Plants should be spaced 2 feet apart. They can be propagated by division in spring.
Uses: Sunny gardens, xeriscapes, groundcover.

Zauschneria californica
'Glasnevin'

PESTS AND DISEASES

Wildflowers and native plants are often touted as the solution to every problem area or as being completely free of pests. This simplistic belief overlooks the many considerations to making a native planting disease free and low maintenance. A key to the success of naturalistic plantings of wildflowers is selecting plants that are right for the site and adapted to its soil and climatic conditions. A plant that is adapted to a garden's particular soil and climatic conditions will be under less stress than something that is growing in a totally inappropriate site. For instance, a cactus will probably die a slow and tortured death when placed in a moist shady location, while the delicate fronds of many fern species will burn when they are grown in too sunny and dry a garden. Plants that are under stress are more likely to succumb to insect and disease problems.

Naturalistic plantings also mimic nature by having a diversity of plant species within a site. By varying the types of plants, you save yourself from the possibility of a single infestation wiping out your entire planting. Instead, you might lose a few plants that are susceptible to that particular pest or disease, but most should be unaffected by the problem. Over the years I have had very few insect or disease problems in my gardens and in my nursery. I credit this to a number of factors:

1. I grow many different kinds of plants; this diversity halts widespread plagues.
2. Consistent use of organic mulches such as shredded bark and leaves makes for a much less stressful environment for the plants. Temperature fluctuations in the soil are moderated, weeds are kept to a minimum, small amounts of nutrients are released by the decomposition of the mulch and earthworm tunnels keep the soil aerated and help to move nutrients down to the root zones.

3. I rarely spray with pesticides and never use herbicides, so my gardens and nursery are teeming with all sorts of wildlife, which helps to keep insect and animal populations in balance. Birds, snakes, toads and predatory insects are all part of nature's pest management system.
4. I don't overfertilize plants. Forcing them to grow too fast puts stress on plants and invites insect and disease problems.

Keep an eye open for any signs of ill health in your plants. Once you have diagnosed the problem, you will have several options for how to deal with it. First you may choose to wait and see what happens. I have found that certain plants (milkweeds, for example) can develop an infestation of orange aphids on the upper stems, yet the plant appears to be unaffected by the insects and the aphids do not move to other plants. In this case I just leave the aphids alone.

Other times, however, a plant is obviously under stress and you will have two alternatives. You can either try to correct the problem quickly by using chemical sprays or you can destroy the plant and thus keep the problem from spreading to other plants. To make this decision you will have to balance the effect of a spray on your own health, the ecosystem of the garden and the value of the plant itself. Often I opt to destroy the plant. If you decide to try a chemical solution, start with one of the relatively nontoxic pesticides or fungicides produced by Safers or Ringers, for instance, that most garden centers and even supermarkets now stock. These are usually soap-based with perhaps an organic insecticide or fungicide included. You should still be careful to read all the directions, avoid breathing any fumes and clean up well after spraying. Try not to spray anywhere near water because you don't want the spray to travel and injure other plants, animals or fish.

The brown cones and reflexed yellow petals of prairie coneflower (Ratibida pinnata) *are supported by fine stems to a height of 4 feet. This plant creates a light and airy effect in the garden.*

POTENTIAL PROBLEMS

Powdery Mildew: A fungal disease easily identified by the powdery white layer that develops on the top of leaves. *Phlox paniculata,* when grown in warm and humid climates, is especially prone to this disease. Powdery mildew does not harm the plant, but it is unsightly and causes lower leaves to drop off. To prevent powdery mildew, place susceptible plants in spots with good air circulation and lots of sun. Infected plants can sometimes be helped by spraying with an organic fungicide.

Aphids: Small insects that can be green, brown, white or orange. They suck the juices from plants and can also spread disease. Outdoors they tend to be less of a problem and they rarely spread with the same vengeance that they do indoors and in greenhouses. If the plant looks stressed, you can spray with an organic soap-based insecticide.

Rabbits and Deer: Although they are adorable, they can wreak havoc on a garden. Cats can be an effective solution to rabbits, and tall, electrified fences will keep all but the hungriest of deer out of the garden. Barring these solutions, I suggest you emphasize plants that rabbits and deer do not find palatable, such as alliums, irises, ferns and grasses. Make sure you talk to other local gardeners and your cooperative extension agent before planting extensive and expensive gardens in areas with deer problems. The information you learn could save you a lot of money and spare you a great deal of disappointment.

Slugs and Snails: Cool, moist and shaded spots are most prone to harboring populations of slugs and snails. This may be one garden site where you want to put down a rougher textured mulch such as sharp pea gravel or even no mulch at all because slugs and snails like to hide under organic mulch. I do not recommend using any chemicals because these poisons are harmful to the toads and birds that naturally keep a snail population under control. Instead, you might try diatomaceous earth, which is a siliceous powder formed by the shells of diatoms, an algae found in the ocean. It is sold in a powdered form. The sharp edges of the diatomaceous earth will cut the soft bodies of snails and slugs and serve as a deterrent to these pests. Because it is fairly expensive and must be reapplied every few weeks in rainy climates, it is best saved for new plantings and young seedlings that might not be able to survive a slug attack. As in the case of deer and rabbit problems, talk to fellow gardeners and try to grow those plants that slugs don't eat, such as wild columbine (*Aquilegia canadensis*), foamflower (*Tiarella cordifolia*) and cardinal flower (*Lobelia cardinalis*).

Japanese Beetles: Bane of the East, these large buzzing beetles emerge in early summer to attack the leaves and flowers of many favorite plants. Rosebuds and blossoms are about the saddest sight in the summer garden when dripping with a mass of these horrible creatures. There are traps that attract beetles using a sex attractant, but it has always seemed to me that the hormone only served to attract many more beetles to a garden than would have been there without the traps. Some people have had success using milky spore, a disease that kills the beetles while they are in their grub cycle. It is applied to lawns, where the grubs live.

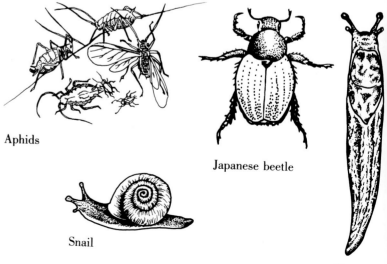

Aphids

Japanese beetle

Snail

Slug

GARDENERS' MOST-ASKED QUESTIONS

Question: What do people mean when they say native plant?
Answer: A native plant is one that evolved naturally in a site without the aid or interference of people.

Question: Why should I grow native plants?
Answer: The key to the health of the earth, as well as our own backyard ecosystems, lies in a diversity of wildlife, whether plant or animal. By growing some plants native to the region where we live, we help retain some of the natural diversity that once existed. Otherwise we run the danger of transforming the United States into a monoculture of forsythia, pachysandra and liriope.

Question: What do the terms naturalized *and* alien species *mean?*
Answer: These terms are used to describe wildflowers that evolved in other parts of the world but were introduced to the United States. Common roadside flowers such as chicory and Queen Anne's lace actually are native to Europe and Asia, but escaped from gardens in this country and have become "naturalized" wildflowers.

Question: Where can I buy wildflowers?
Answer: Many garden centers are now selling wildflowers. Recently there has been an increase in the number of specialty nurseries across the country that will ship wildflowers to your door. Begin by contacting your local botanical garden, wildlife organization and cooperative extension agency for nurseries that emphasize plants appropriate to your region of the country. (See page 91 for a list of nurseries.)

Question: Some nurseries say they sell only "nursery propagated" wildflowers. What does this mean?
Answer: Unfortunately, there are still some nurseries that sell plants collected from the wild. Educated gardeners have become concerned by the fact that these nurseries are depleting natural areas of their diverse and beautiful flowers. An increasing number of growers across the country propagate wildflowers, rather than collect them from the wild, and they proudly announce this fact in their catalogs.

Question: Do nursery propagated plants grow better than those collected from the wild?
Answer: Most of the time, they do. In the wild a plant sends its roots in many different directions, often around rocks and under tree roots. A nursery-grown flower will have a more compact root system because it was grown in a pot or in a carefully prepared nursery bed. The nursery-grown plant will suffer much less stress from being transplanted because most of its roots will not be damaged by the move.

Question: How do I know how long the period of moist, cold stratification should be?
Answer: Most seeds require 4 to 6 weeks of exposure to moisture and 40° to 45° F temperatures. If the temperature is higher or lower, the bacterial and chemical reactions necessary to permit germination will be slowed (and at extremes of warmth or cold, these activities will cease). In a refrigerator, which is usually the perfect temperature, 4 to 6 weeks

should be enough time. When sown outside in cold climates, it is wise to allow seeds to stratify for several months. Freezing temperatures won't hurt the seeds but the stratification process will be slowed or halted. By giving the seeds several months outdoors and allowing the seedlings to germinate with the natural warmth of spring, you will be guaranteed that the seeds have received a sufficient period of stratification without using up the limited space within your refrigerator.

Question: I have an ugly spot on my property that I'd like to turn into a wildflower meadow. How do I go about doing this?

Answer: First you should realize that wildflower meadows are not the low-maintenance, quick-fix solution they were advertised as during most of the 1980s. Researching and establishing a successful meadow takes just as much effort as a similar sized perennial border. More detailed information on meadows is offered in Chapter 2.

Question: What are some wild-flowers that will grow in a dry spot underneath my oak tree?
Answer: *Tiarella cordifolia, Aquilegia canadensis* or *A. formosa* and *Polemonium reptans* would make pretty spring-flowering groundcovers in such a site.

Question: I have a very dry, sunny spot. What are some good drought-tolerant natives?
Answer: The annual California

poppies should grow happily under the conditions you describe. You could also plant some opuntias and yuccas for year-'round interest. Remember that even drought-tolerant plants will need extra water for the first year or two until they have had a chance to become established in a site.

Question: What are some good wildflowers for a spring woodland garden?
Answer: The classic combination of *Aquilegia canadensis, Phlox divaricata* and *P. stolonifera, Stylophorum diphyllum, Tiarella cordifolia, Smilacina racemosa, Polygonatum biflorum* and ferns is still my favorite.

Question: What are some pretty wildflowers for the summer garden?
Answer: *Heliopsis helianthoides, Hibiscus palustris, Monarda punctata* with *Lobelia siphilitica, Monarda didyma* cultivars and *Phlox paniculata* cultivars. All of these look nice highlighted by some graceful grasses such as *Panicum virgatum* or *Sorghastrum nutans.*

Question: Which wildflowers will provide color late into the fall?
Answer: *Chrysopsis villosa* creates a showy gold display late in the season, *Aster novae-angliae* cultivars come in shades of pink, white, lavender and purple, *Lobelia siphilitica* usually keeps on producing blue spikes until frost and many of the grasses turn brilliant shades of copper or red.

Question: What are some wild-flowers that the deer won't eat?
Answer: For those who live where deer grazing is a problem, this answer can often be difficult. When talking to other gardeners you will soon learn that each population of deer has its own preferences and they vary from area to area. It also depends upon the population pressure within a region. If the deer are hungry, they will eat plants that would normally be passed over. As a general rule of thumb, though, deer don't eat grasses, ferns, plants with aromatic foliage and plants with gray leaves.

Question: What are some wild-flowers that rabbits won't eat?
Answer: Rabbits also don't like grasses, ferns, plants with aromatic foliage and plants with gray leaves. If you know you have a rabbit problem you should be aware that they devour the woodland phloxes such as *Phlox divaricata* and *P. stolonifera.* These beauties are so worth having in the shade garden that I am inclined to suggest you adopt a cat. If this is not a viable solution, try growing *Polemonium reptans* instead of the phlox to obtain a foamy blue effect in the spring garden.

Please write or call for a free Burpee catalog:
W. Atlee Burpee & Co.
300 Park Avenue
Warminster, PA 18974
(215) 674-9633

RESOURCE GUIDE

Unless noted, all of these nurseries are mail-order and require a payment of $2 for their catalogs.

Agua Fria Nursery (free catalog)
1409 Agua Fria St.
Santa Fe, NM 87501
Western wildflowers

Eastern Plant Specialities
Box 226
Georgetown, ME 04548
(207) 371-2888
Many plants native to eastern United States

Fancy Fronds
1911 4th Ave. West
Seattle, WA 98119
(206) 284-5332
Specializing in ferns

Foliage Gardens
2003 128th Ave. West
Bellevue, WA 98005
(206) 747-2998
Wide variety of ferns

Greenlee Nursery (price list is free)
301 E. Franklin Ave.
Pomona, CA 91766
(909) 629-9045
Enormous selection of grasses

Hubbard Nursery
RR1, Box 154
Craryville, NY 12521
(518) 851-2195
No mailorder, plants grown in large sizes

Niche Gardens
1111 Dawson Road
Chapel Hill, NC 27516
(919) 967-0078
Southeastern wildflowers, nice catalog

Louisiana Nursery (catalog $3.50)
Rt. 7, Box 43
Opelousas, LA 70570
(318) 948-3696
Huge selection of Louisiana irises

Prairie Moon Nursery
Rt. 3, Box 163
Winona, MN 55987
(507) 452-1362
Seeds and plants of prairie wildflowers

Prairie Nursery
P.O. Box 306
Westfield, WI 53964
(608) 296-3679
Seeds and plants of prairie wildflowers

We-Du Nurseries
Rt. 5, Box 724
Marion, NC 28752
(704) 738-8300
Many unusual southeastern natives

Wildwood, Inc. (catalog $1.00)
Rt. 3, Box 165, Hwy. 64 West
Pittsboro, NC 27312
Hybrid lobelias

THE USDA PLANT HARDINESS MAP OF NORTH AMERICA

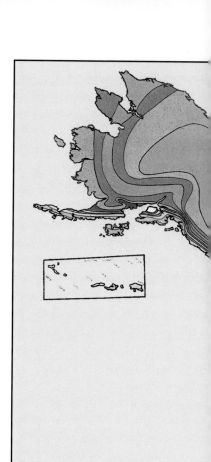

Average Annual Minimum Temperature

Temperature (°C)	Zone	Temperature (°F)
-45.6 and Below	1	Below -50
-45.8 to -45.5	2a	-45 to -50
-40.0 to -42.7	2b	-40 to -45
-37.3 to -40.0	3a	-35 to -40
-34.5 to -37.2	3b	-30 to -35
-31.7 to -34.4	4a	-25 to -30
-28.9 to -31.6	4b	-20 to -25
-26.2 to 28.8	5a	-15 to -20
-23.4 to -26.1	5b	-10 to -15
-20.6 to -23.3	6a	-5 to -10
-17.8 to -20.5	6b	0 to -5
-15.0 to -17.7	7a	5 to 0
-12.3 to -15.0	7b	10 to 5
-9.5 to -12.2	8a	15 to 10
-6.7 to -9.4	8b	20 to 15
-3.9 to -6.6	9a	25 to 20
-1.2 to -3.8	9b	30 to 25
1.6 to -1.1	10a	35 to 30
4.4 to 1.7	10b	40 to 35
4.5 and Above	11	40 and Above

This zone map provides a broad outline of various temperature zones in North America. However, every garden has its own microclimate.

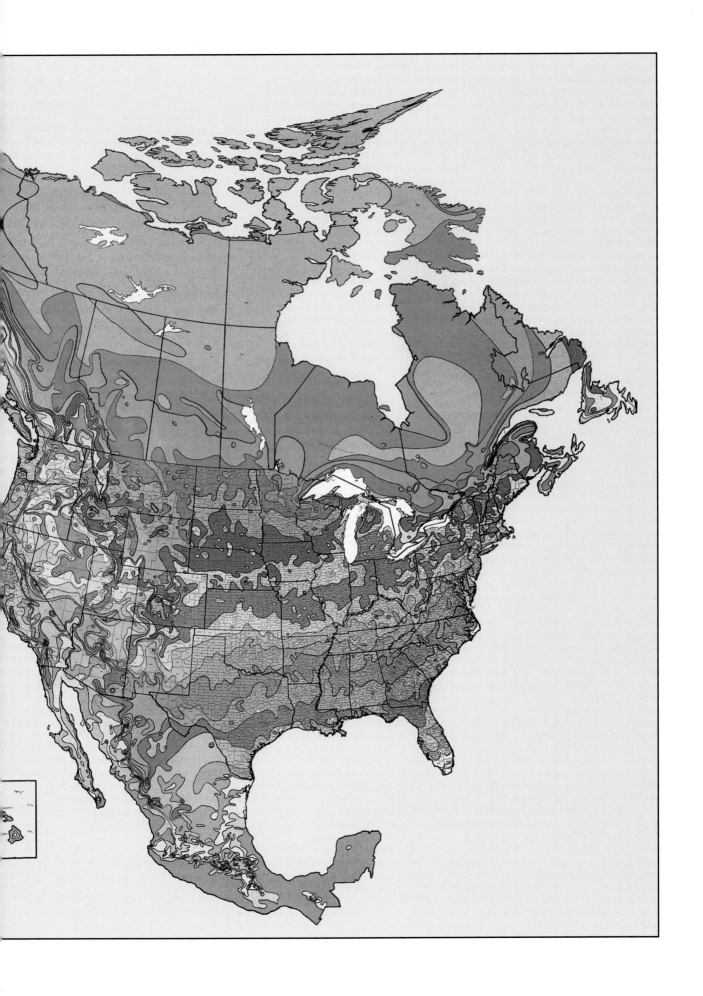

Index

(NOTE: Italized page numbers refer to captions)